When He

*Discovering the Power
of Divine Encounters.*

By
Lucas Sherraden
and
Graham Cooke

**Foreword by
Randy Clark**

When Heaven Opens

Copyright © 2006 by Lucas Sherraden

Requests for information should be addressed to—

Lucas Sherraden
c/o Abiding Life Christian Fellowship
4133 Bluebonnet Drive
Stafford, TX
USA 77477

ISBN Number: 978-1-4276-2322-5
E-mail: info@lucasministries.com
Web site: www.lucasministries.com

Printed in the U.S.A.

<u>Acknowledgements</u>

I want to thank all those who helped make this book possible.

Thanks to my wife, family and friends for your support and love through this process. It is because of what we have together that I am genuinely a wealthy man.

Thanks to the elder team of Abiding Life Christian Fellowship for your support, friendship and commitment. This message could not be what it is without our team being what it is.

Thanks to Dr. Mike Kesner for your prophetic word to write this and for your support.

Thanks to Randy Clark for opening so many doors for me and believing in me.

Thanks to Gary and Kathi Oates for your strategic role in my life and in this experience.

Thanks to Graham Cooke for your enthusiastic encouragement.

Thanks to Catherine French, Lucy Deliganis, Sherry McCollom and Julia Loren – your help in writing and editing was invaluable.

Endorsements

"Just as there are seasons in the natural, so there are in the Spirit. *When Heaven Opens* gives us an indication that the seasons are changing. The hunger for an authentic gospel increases daily, while great courage has caused many to emerge with the willingness needed to confront fear based restrictions in how we do life. Lucas has successfully confronted the lie that applauds us when we have more confidence in the devil's ability to deceive than the Lord's ability to keep us. I am certain that this book will affect you as it did me, and stir you up to pursue all that God has for us."

Bill Johnson
Author of *When Heaven Invades Earth*
Pastor - Bethel Church
Redding, CA

Because supernatural activity is on the increase, *When Heaven Opens* is a timely book. It will create in you a hunger for more of God's presence and a desire for intimacy with Him.

Lucas does a great job of explaining his heavenly encounters in a way that will help you experience more of God's supernatural realm. You will gain valuable lessons and insight from his experiences that can catapult you into your destiny."

Gary and Kathi Oates
Authors of *Open My Eyes, Lord*
Open My Heart, Lord

◆◆◆

When Heaven Opens is a life changing, transforming book.
Lucas and Graham have done an exceptional job. This is not just
a book; it is a supernatural encounter and experience. The truths
revealed will cause a hunger and passion to stir deep within,
resulting in the cry of, "Father, I desire more of You." It will
challenge you to go higher and deeper in intimacy with the Lord
and to press in to all His Kingdom encompasses. As I read, the
anointing began to pour off the pages into my heart and spirit. I
found myself weeping and longing for His presence and more of
the supernatural realm. While at the same time being filled with
hope, joy, faith and an expectancy of the incredible hour of
history in which we live. This book imparts faith and passion to
experience the supernatural and to embrace the process of
becoming all God has created for this day and hour.

Rebecca Greenwood
Author of *Authority to Tread*
President
Christian Harvest International

TABLE OF CONTENTS

Foreword by Randy Clark

Lucas Sherraden's book *When Heaven Opens* (co-authored by Graham Cooke) is an invitation into greater intimacy with God. Drawing upon his own experience with having his eyes opened and seeing into the spiritual dimension of reality, he lays out before each of us the invitation to come closer to God. With insights from the Bible regarding God's heart for His people, and His desire that they walk in power, revelation, wisdom and compassion, Lucas and Graham invite us to pursue what we would historically call revival. With amazing understanding of his own experience, in light of his Baptist commitment to the Word of God, the Bible, this book is an encouragement to experience the "hot fire" of revival. While reading Lucas' book, I could not help but think of other famous evangelists' experiences: John Wesley's experience of feeling his heart strangely warmed within him, D.L. Moody's experience of having so much power going through his body he thought he would die if the experience continued, and Charles G. Finney's experience of seeing the Lord and feeling waves of love and electricity coursing through his body to the point that he, too, thought he would die if they continued.

Lucas received this experience while on one of our Global Awakening teams in Brazil. He became hungry for such an experience with God after hearing Gary Oates share an experience that he, too, had on one of our Global Awakening trips to Brazil a few years earlier. Lucas sought God and God answered his prayer by opening his eyes to see into the spiritual realm. In this experience, God revealed to Lucas one of the major keys to breaking through into revival.

1

I still remember seeing him about five hours after the experience. He was still trembling, heat was still radiating from his body, and he was still undone, barely able to communicate. His eyes filled with tears as he tried to communicate what had happened to him. He had experienced the wonderful terror of being in the presence of God. I encouraged him to write out his experience in great detail and have had him share about it in meetings. Now, after much reflection and biblical analysis of the experience, Lucas is making it available to bless the whole Church.

Lucas is a well-trained Baptist pastor who loves the Word and the Spirit. I believe this book will encourage others to desire revival in their personal lives, their church, their city and their nation. Though born out of experience, this book is about God's desire to consume us with Himself and to breathe upon us His Spirit, allowing us to live in the exciting time of personal revival. It is Lucas' desire that the experience would not end merely in *personal* revival, but in *city transforming* revival. May this book be used to gather the kindling wood of people who likewise have set their hearts on seeing the Kingdom and its King. May those who read this book also meet the one who calls Himself the Captain of the Host, the Ruler of the Kingdom of Heaven and Ruler of the Kingdom of God on Earth!

Introduction

If you are deliriously satisfied with your Christian experience, you have purchased this book to absolutely no avail. It was not written for you.

But…if this book finds you in a place where you really want more out of your relationship with God and are willing to let Him open doors of new possibilities, then this book has the potential to accelerate your Christian walk – maybe in some unexpected ways. Odds are that you have come to this book because you want more of the Lord. Many believers today want more of God, but find themselves in a variety of circumstances. You might be in a place where you are absolutely passionate about your relationship with the Lord Jesus. Then again, you might have a rich history with Christianity and church but currently find yourself not completely satisfied. Or you may be overwhelmed with spiritual boredom but not willing or able to admit that. Another possibility may be that you are reading this with your "theological guard" on "high alert" due to the very theme of this book!

Regardless of your situation, if you read this book carefully with openness to the Lord's voice, consider my experiences and insight in the light of God's Word and receive the Biblical truths contained within these pages, you will find that the embers of **hope** within your heart will be restored. **Hope** that supernatural realties such as third heaven encounters, angelic visitations, and other Scriptural encounters of a spiritual nature are attainable, valuable and potentially strategic for contemporary Christianity. In addition, you will discover very important messages that God is currently communicating to His people.

3

My story is simply that … it's my story. But the phenomenon that I repeatedly witness is that, as I have shared this story in conferences and at churches, the lessons and insights I gained have actually been **transferred** to others. In other words, my testimony becomes a launching pad for others to have similar, and even greater, encounters with God. This has been a great blessing in the lives of many. My vision is that, as these thoughts are read and discussed, increasing numbers of people in the Body of Christ will be launched into experiences just like what they read about in the Scriptures. As people discover the Lord in these types of ways, the revelation that will be released will build faith for this day so that we can accomplish the "greater works" prophesied by the Lord Jesus.

There are those who are new to all of this so allow me to clarify: …**the playing field has been leveled**. If you feel like you will never have a mystical experience like this … I am immensely familiar with that feeling! The truth of the matter is that I really am an extremely atypical candidate to have been graced with this type of an encounter. My life has been pretty "normal" sprinkled with highs and lows like most everyone else. So take comfort!

There is also a group who will read these pages who are very seasoned in the revelatory realms. For you, this book may hold some important keys for processing revelatory experiences in the context of a community of believers in solid friendship. My conviction is that as you read, God's Spirit will strengthen your faith to pursue even more!

When Heaven Opens begins with a masterfully written Prologue by Graham Cooke. It establishes the context for being surprised by God amidst the activity of our lives. Graham insightfully encourages us with keys on handling a *"suddenly of*

God." In an instant, God can change **everything** in our lives…which is precisely what happened to me. The next chapter details my spiritual situation before God took me into this encounter – the "set up." The following chapters express what happened to me in its entirety. Much of how I describe my experience is taken almost verbatim from the journal I wrote within hours of the event. The following few chapters look more carefully at the pieces and elements of the vision, and the possible implications for God's people. I then discuss how this experience has changed my life and ministry. There is a chapter offering keys that helped me process this experience. I am convinced that many more of the Body of Christ are going to experience these types of encounters and will need to know how to process them. Finally, I have included a chapter showing how you can join in what the Lord revealed through my vision and position yourself for your own spiritual encounters.

The tide is turning and the spiritual climate is changing rapidly in this historic moment. So if you are ready to see how the Lord Jesus is impacting the world today thru "everyday Christians," if you are willing to be challenged and stretched by God who is currently restoring the kinds of mystical experiences we read about in the Bible, or if you are just hungry for more Kingdom reality in your life, take this journey with me and let's discover what frontiers are obtainable to you when heaven opens.

Prologue
Suddenly, God!
By Graham Cooke

It was just a normal Friday.

David was up on the hillside of his father's farm, doing what he did everyday: watching sheep graze. All was quiet except for the odd sheepy "bah" and the songs David hummed to himself. The Middle Eastern sun beat down on him. It was hot. Dreadfully hot. It was always ridiculously hot on that hillside.

Not to say there wasn't excitement every once in a while. Six months earlier, a lion had happened upon the happy little flock. Some quick hands and good aim with a slingshot had stopped that threat cold. A few weeks after that, a bear wandered across the hill, looking for lunch. Dave couldn't remember ever seeing a bear in that neighborhood, but he didn't bother to get a life history. He simply pulled out his trusty slingshot, ran toward the bear, and killed it. That was David's job—protecting his father's sheep at all costs.

But other than the occasional bout, it was quiet. Always quiet. Day after day passed in dull succession. To entertain himself, Dave penned poems and songs and taught himself how to play musical instruments. After a few years on the hill, even that grew tiresome.

It was just another normal Friday, and David was bored.

Looking into the valley, David noticed something strange going on at his father's house. Something was happening, but he couldn't make out what. To get a better look,

6

he climbed onto a small cliff and stared down as hard as he could. Servants seemed to be rushing in and out of his father's home, scurrying to get various people and supplies. There seemed to be activity everywhere, but David couldn't discern why.

Just then, he heard a voice calling up the hillside.

"Dave! David!" bellowed one of his father's servants. "Where are you?"

David climbed down from the cliff and met the servant. "What is it?" he asked, bracing the exhausted servant so he wouldn't fall over.

"It's your father, Dave," the servant huffed, barely able to catch his breath. "He wants you to come see him right away. And Dave – be on your best behavior, because Samuel the prophet is there. Jesse'll skin you alive if you misbehave. I'm to stay and watch the sheep, but you need to get down there now."

David made his way down the hill, happy to be leaving the crushing boredom of his sheep-watching routine, but uncertain of what he was walking into. Just outside the house stood his mother, waiting for him with a fresh change of clothes and a damp washcloth.

"What's going on?" asked David, changing into the clean clothes as his mother scrubbed his face.

"Samuel's here," answered his mom. "I don't know why, but he has been asking for each of your brothers to come and see him. Your dad has been in there with him for hours. I don't know what's happening but, David, it's serious." Quickly, she kissed him on the forehead and pushed him into the house.

7

As David stepped through the doorway, a thought occurred to him: *Have I done anything wrong lately that would require the attention of a prophet?* Just then, his father grabbed him around the shoulders and led him into the room, all the while giving him an embarrass-me-and-you'll-be-sorry look. To their left stood David's brothers, lined up from oldest to youngest, and all looking miserable. Only he himself was missing at the end of the line.

And there was Samuel, the most famous man of his time, standing quietly on the other side of the room. David had never seen him before, and was surprised at how short he was: *I pictured him being much taller*, David thought to himself. Samuel's prophecies over the previous decades had shaped Dave's nation and faith. Now the two stood in the same tent— one an elderly, world-renowned prophet, the other a simple, teenaged shepherd. It was intimidating for the teenager, to say the least.

Samuel turned and looked deep into David's eyes. Time seemed to stand still as the elderly man took stock of the teenager before him. David shifted uncomfortably on his feet. *This guy can see right through me,* he thought to himself. *What is going on here?*

"That's him," Samuel announced. "That's the one I've come for. He's the one."

The one what? David thought wildly. *I haven't done anything to merit him coming. Why is he here for me?*

After a moment that seemed like a lifetime, Samuel moved on David, uncorking a flask of oil and pouring it out over the young man's head. In one swift motion, David was anointed king, in time, over Israel.

Suddenly, this Friday was different from any other Friday of his life.

What do you do when God suddenly changes everything? How do you stand when you receive a prophetic word declaring a future that is absolutely incredible, but totally remote from where you are now? What are you supposed to do? What do you say? How do you respond? What kind of thoughts do you have in that blink of an eye when everything changes?

How do you live with a "suddenly" – a moment when God suddenly changes your whole outlook on life? What happens when a change happens that you simply cannot articulate to others?

In a "suddenly," God invades our lives in such a way that it excites us on one level and frightens us on another. We become a walking paradox: everything has changed, yet everything is the same.

Suddenly, everything had changed for David. His father hugged him, but it was different: it was as though David was fragile somehow. There was affection in the embrace, but there was also apprehension about what was to come. Jesse, usually so confident and direct, seemed at a loss over what to do next. His brothers, meanwhile, could barely make eye contact with him; they were obviously disappointed by Samuel's choice.

"Well," his father said quietly after a few minutes, "I guess you need to get back up the hill to watch the sheep."

9

"Yes sir," David murmured, stumbling out of the house and into his mother's arms.

"What happened?" she asked, taking a towel and wiping the oil from his face.

"Samuel just anointed me to be king over Israel," David answered quietly.

"What?"

"I'm not kidding around, Mom. Samuel just anointed me to be king."

"Well, what are you going to do now?" she asked, perplexed.

"I'm going back up the hill," he said. "I've got to watch the sheep."

As David walked back up the hill, his thoughts were all over the map. On one level, nothing had changed. He was still in charge of his father's flock, protecting it from danger, and yet everything had changed. It was a normal day, except that a "suddenly" had made an appearance in his life – and completely wrecked it. What do you do after this kind of day?

In counseling, it is one battle to get free and a quite different battle to stay free. We all know people who have become free of something by divine intervention but did not take that release to a new dimension of life. They failed the process that came after the victory.

Similarly, in warfare, we face one fight to take ground and a different fight to hold on to that territory. The object of victory is occupation of territory. The second battle is designed to establish the victory and take possession of the ground.

In a "suddenly" it is one thing to say "yes" with excitement to the possibilities that are being declared over you. It is quite another thing to say yes to the process that comes with it.

A "suddenly" plunges us into a great internal process. In this place we need to adjust our thinking, perceiving and obedience. We must become more sensitive to the Holy Spirit. Over time, our character, faith, personality and anointing need to move to a higher level of intentionality. Our whole relationship with God must move into a new realm of expression.

The person we are now internally must go through a process of adjustment and development. We now must walk out of who we are to become involved with the new person that comes from the future and that needs to emerge in our lifestyle.

Many thoughts ran through David's head. He pictured himself inside a palace, wearing a kingly robe. He thought of the money and treasure and glory that came with being king. He thought of the fame and power he would soon wield. But doubts plagued him, too. *We have a king, and he's not my father. How can I be king? What kind of man am I going to need to be in order to lead properly? What does a king even do all day? Will I have to learn how to command an army? How do I do that? Will I have to build schools and roads and hospitals and defenses? Why did Samuel pick me? And why now? Why not one of my brothers? They, at least, have military experience. Me? I'm just a shepherd. Who on earth would ever follow me?*

Dave's family fought similar thoughts. In a heartbeat, family relationships had become awkward. *What do we say to him? How do we interact with a future king? When we sit down*

11

for a family meal, how will we treat him? His brothers were a mess: *How can I look at him without measuring him? I'm a better fighter than he is. I'm a better speaker. I'm smarter. I'm better-looking. I'm taller. Why Davey?*

All of them – dad, mom, the brothers, even the servants – had questions for David, but the young man had no answers for any of them. His parents wondered how they would discipline a future king. *Can we still send him to his room? Do we let him go find his own way?* Everyone had questions, but there were very few answers.

A "suddenly" provokes us to think about ourselves in a completely different way than ever before. A whole new area has opened up in front of us and we have to go and explore it – but we have no idea where to even start.

Over the next few weeks, David began to come to terms with what God was doing. He slowly generated a standard of thinking that put him in line with what God had called him to do. Little did he know during that season how important this new way of thinking was going to be.

One day, Jesse asked David to take some food to his brothers, who had been called up to fight the Philistine army. They had been out there for a while, and Jesse wanted to make sure they had a good meal before the battle picked up.

"Take this food to your brothers," Jesse said. "And come straight back, Dave. No messing around."

David arrived at his brothers' camp just in time to witness the biggest man he had ever seen challenge the Israelites. As Goliath taunted his countrymen, something stirred inside the future king. *This guy is challenging something that's going to be mine some day,* David thought to himself. *So who is going to answer this giant?* Imagine his disappointment when no one – not the current king, not a general, not even the brothers he looked up to—came out to meet Goliath's challenge. *If we're not careful,* David thought, *we're going to lose this kingdom before I inherit it.*

David looked across at the giant. Anger rose up within him: *What nerve this guy has, flinging out curses against my country and my God! And no one in all Israel will stand up to this man?*

So the teenager starting asking the question that the more experienced warriors should have been pondering. "What will be done for the man who takes out this giant?" David asked it boldly and repeatedly, as veteran warriors looked away sheepishly. Others snickered at the young pup's desire to be killed. But Dave would not shut up, kicking up such a fuss that he eventually ended up before the king.

Imagine that meeting for just a moment. It was probably the first time he had ever seen the king up close and personal. Saul may have been sitting on a throne, wearing royal robes and ordering servants around. What must have been running through David's mind? *This will be mine some day. That throne, this army, that ring, those servants, that robe, that footstool, everything. Well, maybe I'll get a better footstool; that one is kind of ugly. Still, it will all be mine – I better make sure it sticks around in the meantime.*

13

"If no one else will face this giant, I will," David told the king. Out of nowhere came servants with armor and a sword. They dressed Dave in full battle gear; the poor lad couldn't even move. *This isn't me,* he thought. *I can't fight like this.* He stripped the armor off and walked the perimeter of the camp. *What is it I need to win this fight? This Goliath has four brothers. I guess I better take five rocks in case I need to kill 'em all.*

Finally the moment came. David stood alone in front of his nation's mightiest warriors and answered Goliath's challenge. But he had more than just a slingshot and five rocks with him in this fight – he had a promise from God. He knew he couldn't die, because he had a prophetic word about being king. God had a plan for his life, and not even a giant could stand in its way. There is little doubt about what David was thinking in that moment: *It sucks to be you right now, Goliath. One of us is going to die, but it can't be me. I have a prophecy from Sam that hasn't been fulfilled yet. But you, you have nothing to stand on. Dude, you are soooo dead!*

Goliath looked at David with contempt. "I'm going to feed your body to the beasts of the field and the birds of the air," the Philistine roared.

"Is that right?" responded Dave. "Well, I'll feed you – and all your friends, too! How do you like those apples?" Immediately, David ran towards Goliath. With no fear of losing, he charged the giant and engaged him on his own terms. This was a winnable fight. Killing the lion and the bear on his father's hillside had taught him what the power of God felt like and what it could accomplish.

14

Pulling his slingshot out, he fired a stone into Goliath's forehead. The giant, stunned, fell to the ground. David unsheathed Goliath's sword and killed him. David took the very thing the enemy was going to use to kill him and ended the threat.

Suddenly, David, the unknown teenage shepherd, was catapulted to national fame. Just like that, one "suddenly" of God had come on top of another. The women sang songs about him: "Saul has killed his thousands, and David his tens of thousands!" Children pretended to be him while they played on the hillsides and streets of Israel: "No, it's my turn to be David!"

"Suddenlies" occur when God swoops down, picks us up, and deposits us in a higher place than we have ever been before. In the time that follows, we have to develop the disciplines to stay there. We must learn to abide in God at a higher level.

I have always found it interesting that Christians spend so much time and energy praying for an immediate move of God, when God will never do something that takes away the need for process and discipline. We always get to work out, and walk out, our salvation in fear and trembling. Even if God suddenly picks us up and deposits us at a higher level, we still have the process and discipline of learning how to live there in that place.

In life, either our process and discipline gets us into a new call, or it is the thing that keeps us there if God takes us up in an outrageous move of the Spirit. "Suddenlies" do not save us from process, but they do accelerate our learning. In a season of divine acceleration – which is what happens when a suddenly

15

occurs – what we think will take years to occur takes months. What we think will take months, takes weeks. What we think will take weeks, takes days. What we think will take days, takes hours, and what we think will take hours, takes moments. The gap between prophecy spoken and prophecy fulfilled gets narrower. We are coming to a day, not too far off, when prophecy spoken in the morning will be fulfilled in the afternoon. I believe we will see a release of Genesis 1-type prophecy: "Let there be" words. Things will be created as soon as we prophesy them.

Truth be told, the vast majority of Christians feel as though they are lagging behind the timeline of their own spiritual development. I hear it again and again in churches around the world: "I should be further on than I am right now." This is not condemnation; our journey is our journey. But we have some catching up to do as individuals to get to where God wants us to be. Fortunately, the grace of God enables us to do just that. God wants to redeem time because the days are evil – and getting worse.

It was just a normal Tuesday.

Moses was alone, out in the desert, working just as he had worked every day for the past several years. It was stinking hot, as usual, but he had long since become used to the heat, sun and dust. In fact, Moses had lost count of the number of times he had seen small bushes spontaneously combust because of the heat. The first time had scared him, but he knew now what a common occurrence it was for a small tree to erupt in flame.

But this Tuesday wasn't like every other Tuesday.

As Moses worked, he saw out of the corner of his eye a whoosh of flame. *There goes another one*, he thought to himself, glancing over. Yet something was different about this one. He couldn't take his eyes off of it. There was something different about this bush fire. There was no smoke. *How can that be?* Moses wondered. *How can a bush be on fire but not burn?* Intrigued, Moses went to take a closer look.

As he approached the bush, something even more incredible happened: the bush spoke.

"Moses, take your shoes off," the bush said. "This is holy ground."

This bush isn't just talking to me – it's giving me orders, Moses thought to himself. After taking a quick look around to make sure this wasn't some sort of family practical joke, Moses took his sandals off and stood before the bush.

Suddenly, Moses' life was turned upside-down. The bush had an assignment for him that would change everything.

In the next few hours, Moses listened with equal amounts of excitement and trepidation as suddenly he is given a call unlike anything he has ever heard of before.

Going back to Egypt was very low on Moses' life to-do list. After all, it was the most occult nation on the face of earth. On top of that, he was a convicted murderer who had been exiled from that country. And even worse than that, the Pharaoh – the most despotic ruler imaginable – was his adopted brother, and was ashamed by Moses' actions. *Been there, done that*, Moses thought. *Just when I've left all that behind, just when I've had my last counseling session, after I've just gotten free from the pain of that old life, this bush sends me back.*

17

A knot was forming in Moses' stomach.

A "suddenly" moment with God can bring out all of our anxieties and insecurities. Quite often, God will call us back into the very thing we have walked out of. Just as David used Goliath's own sword against him, God will give us as a weapon the very issue that the enemy planned to use to snuff us out. Our history is a clue to our destiny.

When God moves us to a higher level, our identity is challenged. We are no longer who we thought we were. We are certainly not who others perceive us to be. A suddenly moment eradicates any opportunity for incremental growth. We don't have five years to subtly mature into it; a suddenly happens immediately and we have to learn how to relate to the Holy Spirit in a new way!

When God suddenly moves, we are put into a position that we often have no desire to be in. Our world is shaken to pieces. Sometimes the change can be so huge that it is actually quite frightening. "Here am I, but send him instead," we find ourselves wanting to say.

Moses stood dazed before the burning bush. The bewilderment on his face was evident.

"Moses, what's that in your hand?" the bush asked.

"A staff," he answered.

"Throw it on the ground."

18

Moses dropped the staff and recoiled in horror as it turned into a snake.

"What are you doing?" Moses asked incredulously.

"I turned your stick into a snake," the bush answered matter-of-factly.

"I can see that! Turn it back!"

"Just pick it up, and it will return to its original form," the bush said.

"I don't want to pick it up! The end with all the teeth is looking at me and licking its lips! You pick it up! I'm not picking it up!"

Eventually Moses worked up the courage to grab the snake. Immediately it turned back into his staff.

"I'm just trying to show you that there is power available to you," the bush said.

"Well, keep your power to yourself, eh," Moses replied.

"Come on, one more, just so you're convinced. Put your hand into your jacket," the bush ordered.

"Okay," Moses said, "but no more snakes."

Moses put his hand into his jacket and then took it back out. He looked at it and couldn't even recognize it as his own. It was white with leprosy and decay.

"AAAAARGGHH!" he screamed. "My hand! What have you done to my hand?" Moses thrust his hand back into jacket; instantly, it was healed.

19

A "suddenly" can plunge us into great internal process. It challenges our present identity. "Who am I?" Moses had an identity crisis because of the event and the calling that came with it. In Exodus 7:1, God makes this remarkable statement, "See, I make you **as** God to Pharaoh, and your brother Aaron shall be your prophet."

"Listen, Moses, you need to see something about yourself, otherwise, you won't be able to do what I have called you to do," God, through the burning bush, said. "Moses, by the time we are finished with Pharaoh, the only way he is going to be able to view you is to think you are some kind of god in human form."

Immediately, Moses knew the ramifications from such a statement. In Egypt, every citizen and slave was taught that Pharaoh was a god. The one true God planned to shake that occult belief to its core.

"I need you to see this, Moses," the bush continued. "When you stand before Pharaoh, you cannot stand as someone inferior or as someone who is on the same level. No, I need you to stand there as someone who is superior to him and as someone who has the power to back up what you're saying. Moses, it's going to be you and Me against all of them."

When God brings a "suddenly" into our lives, our whole perspective must change. We have to see ourselves at a completely different level. Such an upgrade can be difficult, but it is helped by our friends and loved ones. When we are prophetic for one another, we are able to see where God is taking a person.

20

The person you are now must accept the process to become the person you are called to be in the future.

A prophet understands that God is present-future with His people. He is never present-past, because He has already dealt with our past. Jesus has already died for the past. The cross is there to cover it. To be saved, we have to deal with our past and leave it there. God looks at us and says, "I know the plans I have for you, for your welfare, not your calamity, to give you a future and a hope."[1]

Being present-future means we are coming to terms with the actual of who we are and we are dealing with the potential of who we are becoming. When prophecy comes into our life, God is at the potential end of the spectrum, looking ahead, and saying, "This is who you are in the future. I see this." But we hear that voice in the present and all too often dismiss it, looking into a mirror and saying skeptically, "That would take a miracle."

Prophecy opens up a pathway between the actual and the potential. All prophets live in that space in-between. True friends live in that space for each other, because while they can see who we are right now, they also know who we are becoming. In reality, we ought to have two relationships with our friends: one with who they are now, and one to encourage the development and emergence of who they are called to be.

We speak to the present and to the future, bringing those elements together. Prophecy is launched into that gap, opening up a pathway to walk between the two. When God speaks about our future, it is as though the Holy Spirit wraps a silk thread around that future person, brings it to the present, and ties it

---

[1] Jeremiah 29:11

21

around our waist. We have a link between who we are now and who we are called to be. As we follow that rope into our future, we walk through a journey of moving toward the fulfillment of that prophecy. The people who love us should encourage us to work our way along that rope.

In our conversations with each other, we should not simply focus on who we are now, but we should look at who we will be in the future. Sometimes, we have to step into our friend's life and call them to that future standard: "Graham, you cannot do this now, because it doesn't line up with who you are becoming," a friend might say. "If you carry on doing this now, the person that is emerging within you will be hindered."

The calling that comes with a "suddenly" makes our life impossible, unless we change. A "suddenly" provokes inadequacy and is designed to enable us to become dependent on God.

A "suddenly" is a powerful shortcut into a whole new identity; new life; new level; new world. A "suddenly" can be tough. It's a lot of adjustment in a relatively short time frame.

A "suddenly" comes and accelerates this whole process. We need to seriously readjust what we are going to be for one another. We have to make the jump to seeing who our friends are becoming more quickly than ever before. We must relate to that new person much more quickly and powerfully than we would normally react to change. When a friend walks off the map of what they know, we have no right to be antsy about it. Instead, we should recognize the journey they are on, and that it is being accelerated. In that season, we need to learn to run into the future with a new perspective of one another's call and gifts.

It is vital that we reject feelings of jealousy and envy when someone else has a "suddenly" moment with God. Yes, "suddenlies" make things awkward at first, but it is important to get past that. Sudden moves of God change relationships, which means we will need to reinvent our friendships. As God leads us into this age of divine acceleration, it is incumbent upon us to make rapid adjustments. We are all yearning for God to do something incredible in our time. I believe our desperation has reached the point of asking God to do whatever He wants, however He wants it.

Quite simply, a sudden moment with God puts us into a dimension of life for which we are not equipped. We are thrust into a new experience and activity.

We must deal with our procrastination in order to move with new purpose. The only way to do this is to develop a better relationship with the Holy Spirit. Moses has, between the burning bush and the time it took to reach Pharaoh's court, to process who he is in God.

He cannot stand before Pharaoh as anything less than his equal. He cannot show fear or inadequacy. He has to come into the situation at a level of power that is above Pharaoh. "I will make you as God to a god."

He has an accelerated learning opportunity in order to develop the language, persona and mindset of someone who is not inferior.

"Suddenlies" are about divine acceleration and learning how to run. When God deposits us somewhere further and higher than we have ever been, we have to grow up quickly. A "suddenly" catapults us into a different realm of response. To survive there, we must have a transformed heart. It propels us into a different mentality, so we need a new mindset about ourselves. It leads us into a new way of being and a new persona.

Our lives should be guided by two things: who God is and what He is doing in us right now. Who are we? Who are we becoming? We are moving into a time of incredible acceleration when "suddenlies" will be a part of our lives – whether we are ready for them or not. This is the season God has declared. He will change who we are and everything we are doing.

It was just a normal Wednesday.

Like every Wednesday, her son was planning to come by for their regular lunch date. He made sure he spent every Wednesday afternoon with her. He had always been a good boy, and, now, at age 25, he was an even better man. Ever since he had been old enough to walk, she, along with his grandmother, his older sisters, and his aunts, had doted on him. He had been the apple of their eye. As he had gotten older, they had scoured the countryside looking for the perfect girl for him to settle down with. These women had whittled down every family in the region, leaving just a handful for him to select from. He deserved the best, and she, his mother, was going to make sure he got just that.

Suddenly, the door opened, and her son, Hosea, arrived for lunch. Little did she know that nothing was ever going to be the same again.

24

"Mom," he said, "I've got some news. God has told me that I'm going to marry a prostitute."

Hosea's mother was stunned. Angry, she called his father to come into the room. The two of them ordered, demanded, cajoled and begged Hosea to change his mind.

"You'll ruin our family's reputation. We'll be a laughing stock."

"You deserve so much better."

"Why, Hosea? Why?"

The afternoon wore on but Hosea remained resolute. Desperate, his mother called all of the religious leaders and experts she could think of. Surely the boy would listen to one of them.

"How can this be God?"

"God wants you to be happy and live a pure life."

"That's not God."

"God wouldn't ruin your life like this."

"We've been praying for you for years. We know what He wants for you."

"God doesn't do this kind of thing."

Nothing they could say would change the young man's mind. He was resolved to follow God's will for his life and become a sign to the nation, no matter the cost to himself or to his family. He was sacrificing everything to embrace the suddenly God had sent him.

A "suddenly" can mess with people's theology of what is right and proper, decent and in order. A "suddenly" does not respect the people who are around us. It can mess with everyone's comfort zone. It can embarrass people. It may cause some distress. It can be awkward, uncomfortable. It may interfere with the mindset of people around us. It is hard to understand logically.

At Pentecost[1] everyone was together in one place when suddenly there comes from heaven a noise like a violent rushing wind that fills the whole house. Tongues of fire start resting on people and they are filled with the Holy Spirit and begin speaking in tongues and other languages.

Reaction? On one level, amazement, astonishment! There was great perplexity: "How can this be?" Trying to understand a move of God logically is like trying to catch the wind and put it in a bottle!

Eventually, perplexity may lead to mockery if the answers we want are not forthcoming. If the gospel is foolishness to some, the moving of the Holy Spirit will also be. Mockery, derision and sarcasm are soon followed by accusation. In this case the only logical answer to a spiritual phenomenon is: "They must be drunk."

Why drunkenness? Because the disciples were laughing, shouting and reeling about. Clearly they are under the influence of something (not Someone!) that had intoxicated them.

The Presence of God is like that! So powerful we will need new bodies just to live with Him forever, because His effect on our current bodies always has us falling over! At the

---

[1] Acts 2

26

dedication of the temple when God showed up, not a single person was left standing.

It was just a normal Thursday.

Mary was at home on her couch, thumbing through bridal magazines, and watching 'A Wedding Story' on television. Weddings were constantly on her mind these days. A few weeks before, her boyfriend Joseph had proposed, and Mary was busy preparing for her big moment. She had been down to the shops to register and to look at dresses, and had begun asking friends to be her bridesmaids.

Flipping through the magazine, her eyes fell on the perfect tuxedo for her fiancé. *Joe would look so good in this*, she thought to herself. Joseph was a good man, handsome and kind. He ran a small carpentry business and had quickly fallen in love with Mary. Her friends had known after their first date that the two of them were going to end up together. It was destiny. They were made for each other.

Everyone in town was excited for the wedding. Mary couldn't take two steps in the village without someone stopping her with a "Congratulations!" or wanting to look at her ring. Mary knew that in just a few months, she would be Mrs. Joseph, and she was ecstatic. *My dreams are finally coming true,* she thought. *This is going to be great.*

Suddenly, Gabriel, God's angelic messenger, appeared in Mary's living room. And on this otherwise normal Thursday, Gabriel made an astounding announcement, declaring Heaven's game plan to Mary.

"You will be the mother of the Savior of the world," the angel said matter-of-factly.

Mary was stunned. *How do I react to this?* she asked herself. *Do I thank him? What do I say?*

"How will this happen?" Mary asked, pointing out that she was a virgin, thus ruling out the possibility of a baby.

"Well, the power of God is going to overshadow you, and you will conceive," Gabriel replied.

Mary's mind was racing. *Pregnant? Me? How do I tell my mom and dad? How do I tell Joseph? What do I say? But how I can refuse this? It's God!*

"Be it unto me, according to your word," Mary said. Gabriel vanished.

Some time later, Mary and Joseph were out for lunch together.

"Joe, I have something to tell you," Mary said hesitantly. "This isn't easy. I'm not quite sure how to say it, so I'll just come out with it."

"Okay," said Joseph.

"Well, um, I'm, ah, pregnant – and, uh, it's God," Mary said.

"It's who? You're what?"

"I'm having a baby, and it's going to be the Savior of the world," she answered. "I had a funny experience with God. An angel told me all about it. I'm pregnant. It's going to be the

Savior of the world and … and … and you're not happy, are you?"

"That would be a huge understatement. Of course I'm not happy!" Joseph bellowed.

"My folks said the same thing," Mary said quietly, tears in her eyes. "I'm pregnant. It's God. It truly is, Joe. It really is!"

Joseph's life would never be the same. This ordinary lunch suddenly felt like the worst moment of his life.

Depending on the quality of our inner life, a "suddenly" will leave us feeling either excited and a little apprehensive (normal) or overwhelmed, exposed and frightened.

A "suddenly" has other people saying, "That's not God. He wouldn't do that! He wouldn't make a virgin pregnant and cause her fiancé huge problems!"

A sudden moment with God doesn't just interrupt our own world; it changes things for the people around us, too. It affects our family, our friendships, and the people we work with. Unfortunately, there is no how-to manual published when a "suddenly" occurs. God doesn't drop a teaching CD from Heaven for us to use to convince others of our calling. The Holy Spirit does not publish a pamphlet on how to help relationships through this type of transition.

"Suddenlies" usually bring equal amounts of pain and pleasure. Life is new, awkward, different. Human hopes and dreams may have to fall by the wayside in light of a new thing. God's outrageous plan for our lives can be hard for others to accept.

29

We can never be fully ready for a "suddenly." By its very definition, it has to take us completely off-guard. We cannot anticipate or prepare for it; it just happens because of a sovereign act of God. They are inconvenient. They are hard to believe. "Suddenlies" do not respect us, our present mindset, or the people around us.

Joseph had to be told in a dream to "marry the girl." Being engaged to someone means that you have found your true love and there is no-one else. It is a time of preparation for a life together. God interrupts that process with His own agenda.

Mary and Joseph have to find a new way of being together. How does Joseph treat this woman who has changed so much and who will change even more after the birth of the Savior?

"Suddenlies" mean adjustments for everyone around us, whether they like it or not! If they are going to have a life together, Joseph has to change as much as Mary, otherwise their relationship is just not possible at the new level to which God has introduced them.

Imagine being so confused and appalled at events that you have to be told in a dream what to do about the person you love. Then you have a straight choice. Do I receive that? Do I believe it? If so, how do I live with it? What changes must I make within myself to accommodate what God is doing with the person I love?

The alternative is to reject what is happening. Do I call my beloved back to our previous lifestyle? Forget this ever happened? Do I now face the possibility of losing the person I love? Do I give them an ultimatum, it's either me or what you think is God? Do we go for counseling?

All Mary can do is say "yes" to the Lord and live with the anomaly that her decision creates. What would a church leader say to Mary at this point? What would a counselor's advice be to Mary and Joseph? If Pentecost had happened at a men's retreat, what would church leaders be saying, especially if they were not present? If Pentecost had happened at a women's meeting, what would the leadership's and their husband's reaction be to such a phenomenon?

A "suddenly" commits us to a lifestyle and a calling that will severely test the relationships around us. Changes will clearly have to be made in those relationships if we are to accommodate the will of God. If those relationships cannot adjust, we may have to move on or come to a real understanding of how we can live happily with this new mindset and anointing from heaven.

It is usually the person who has experienced the "suddenly" who is challenged to step back from it, rather than others being encouraged to step up. It is quite impossible to deny a touch from heaven. Normal has just gone to a whole new level. To step back from heaven's touch is to go into an abnormal place. The old place now no longer exists and it cannot be reclaimed. We must go on into what God has opened up or live with the bitter taste of disappointment. We will be forever wondering about what our life would be like if we had gone forward. That kind of strain on a relationship can be huge.

A "suddenly" coming into a relationship creates a paradox; i.e., two opposing ideas contained in the same truth about God. Two conflicting experiences in the same space.

"Suddenlies" will cause us to make some fairly massive adjustments in our lives. We have to re-evaluate everything we are and all that we have in our current relationships.

"Suddenlies" mean acceleration. Fast growth and quick response. A "suddenly" comes with a window of opportunity that renders procrastination redundant. It is the moment to redeem time – not continue wasting it. We have to cut things out of our lives that are no longer necessary or are inappropriate for this new season.

It is a time for God, family and friends. The Lord must be our recreation in this new place to enable us to become familiar with life at a different level. It is a time for relationships to be refreshed. We must pursue thanksgiving and intimacy both in God and one another. We must declare what we most value and appreciate in one another so that our thanksgiving is both vertical to God and horizontal to the people we love. We must pursue our relationships with more openness and intentionality.

Create time and space to develop character and identity. We need to make space to free ourselves up to run the race differently. We must understand the impact on our life and the relationships around us.

If we are to be truly prophetic people, these are days when we will need to be out front, leading something. These are days when we don't simply prophesy something, but we put up our hand and say, "Father, if You want to use me as a visual aid, I'm available." God wants the luxury of knowing that He has thousands of people saying, "If You want to touch me in that way, I give You permission to mess with my life to achieve Your own purpose."

The truth is that God already owns us. He bought us with the Cross, and we belong to Him. The quickening spirit and divine acceleration of a "suddenly" comes on the back of obedience and cooperation. God loves to see His children motivated by His hold on our hearts. When He can see the surrender in us, He adds a quickening spirit to enable us to make up for lost time.

God's blessing comes because of the process we are in, and not instead of it. Therefore it's important that, in our relationship with the Holy Spirit, we allow Him to teach us how to look into the realm of the spirit. We must learn to see "suddenlies" the way God sees them; otherwise our advice to our friends and loved ones will not be sound.

Christians should not be in the business of rescuing one another, because God is not interested in rescuing us. Instead, He is out to transform us by engineering situations in which He can change us. This is why a "suddenly" is such a powerful tool – it forces us to change quickly.

God will not rescue us from something that He spent months plotting to get us into. We must remember that instead of measuring time, God measures growth. The best thing we can do in a "suddenly" moment is cooperate with Him. The sooner we surrender to what He has called us to be, the better off we will be. We must reject the idea of thinking in terms of days or weeks or months or hours and instead think in terms of maturity and surrender. We must think in spiritual ways, not natural ways.

In our relationship with the Holy Spirit, there is an anointing to detect the hand of God at work. What is the Father doing? What is He addressing in you through these circumstances? How should you align yourself with Him? How do you position yourself before Him? What does He expect from you right now? What is it He is trying to change in you? How can you cooperate with the Holy Spirit? How can you work out your salvation?

Despite all of the baggage and work that comes with accepting a "suddenly," it is an easy choice to make. Many Christians have lost the grace to live the way they live at the moment. When we begin to feel as though something new has to happen spiritually in our lives, it may be that God has penciled us in for a "suddenly." The Lord has a plan for our lives.

A sudden moment with God transforms us from being foot soldiers into warriors, prompting us to fight at a higher level than we have ever fought. We are propelled into a place of faith where we will have to very quickly learn to live.

Fortunately, we have a helper in these moments. The Holy Spirit is brilliant at equipping us to deal with "suddenlies" and their aftermath. God is looking for people who will cooperate with Him at an outrageous level, and He will help us succeed in that new place. His commitment to us is eternal, no matter how poorly equipped we are for the new thing. In fact, the worse off we are, the more He wants to use us, for the less of His glory we can claim.

We should ask God for a sudden moment with Him. Smart Christians have already discovered that they are paying a price for not doing anything; why not pay the price and do something remarkable for the Kingdom?

This is a new day in the Spirit. "Suddenly" moments with God change everything. They act as a catalyst to change us and everyone and everything we touch. So many believers are tired of the status quo. We need to call on God to do something new with us. We can no longer live in the place we are at. We long for more – now.

God sets aside people willing to follow His commands at all costs. We can be marked for something extravagant and extraordinary. In an instant, we can be transformed from people who tell other people's stories into the individual that everyone tells tales about.

Jesus Christ deserves excellence from His followers. Whatever He wants, however He wants it, whenever He wants it – we must say yes to His call. While we cannot manufacture a sudden moment with God, we can choose to prepare for it by laying down our baggage and hurts from the past. We can ask forgiveness and repent for what we have done wrong. We can work on our spiritual maturity, dwelling on Scripture and worshipping Him. We can learn how to run quickly in the things of the Holy Spirit by keeping close to His heart. We need to know how to rest in Him, and how to declare what He is doing. God will create a beautiful, undeniable radiance in the hearts of people who say yes to Him.

And no day will ever be ordinary again.

Chapter 1
A Divine "Set Up"

Do not fear, little flock, for it is your Father's good pleasure
to give you the kingdom.
Luke 12:32

It began as just a normal Wednesday.

An angel, a sword, supernatural fire, a soundless roar, a glimpse of the Lord Jesus, Himself – astonishing supernatural experiences came unexpectedly into my life and left me breathless and exhausted, but also spiritually and emotionally changed forever. However, because genuine encounters with an infinite eternal God raise more questions than they answer, I was also plunged into the wonderful world of mystery. Totally surprised by God, I was launched, along with many others who have heard this story, into a new realm of mystery and supernatural living. This journey is another testimony of the God who has been called jokingly "Jehovah-sneaky," the Lord who surprises us! ***And in this moment of history, there is an open invitation for believers to enter into heavenly mysteries previously not accessible.***

For years, I sang along to the deafening chorus of the American church, **"Lord - there just HAS to be more!"** This is a cry heard from the depths of many well meaning, works-weary churchgoers who are privately questioning and secretly bored with "church." Guilt, shame and external religious obligation keeps us routinely attending weekly meetings, but under the surface, we still harbor hope that we are destined for greatness and ache for so much more.

Perhaps, for a variety of reasons, you may have even given up on church, organized religion and any other expressions of faith. Perhaps you are still involved. Regardless, within the depths of your heart you have not abandoned the idea of a supernatural God. Not yet. **This book is for those who feel the ache of their destiny of greatness**. Deep within you know it – there just has to be more.

After a lifetime of attending church, preaching and vocational ministry, the possibility that there actually *WAS* more became more than a whimsical desire for me – it became a terminal heart condition. Despite years of serving God as a pastor, I yearned for more than what I had personally experienced and wondered if I would ever be satisfied. It is not a good situation when the pastor is bored at church! Without knowing it, this unarticulated dissatisfaction was setting me up for a sudden experience with God– an encounter of Biblical proportions. God carefully orchestrated events in my life, and the encounter was so profound that, not only has it transformed my own life, it is opening the door for many others to enjoy deep and transforming experiences with God.

The Creator has deposited a seed within us that will only be satisfied with deeper spiritual realities – with more of Him. Because we are created in God's image, it is lethal to remain steeped in the quagmire of a system that does not inspire any hope for greatness. After these experiences, I am certain that we don't have to settle for status quo and spiritual mediocrity. There really are deeper realms of God that He wants us to experience!

This book is not just one man's experience with God; it can become part of an answer to all men and women of destiny who are crying out for more. It is meant to prepare anyone to receive deeper revelation – for ourselves and for our communities. It is an invitation to greater depths and the fulfillment of our God-given desire for supernatural reality that will cure our spiritual boredom. I share it in hopes that courage will steady your heart in your pursuit for more of God's Kingdom.

I was born into a nice, middle class family and raised in Kansas. My mother is Korean, my father is American. My sister and I were raised under the comforting routines of school and church. For me, ministry was my only career choice. I started preaching when I was 16. Much to my delight, many teenagers received Christ. During this time, I developed an insatiable desire to see more of God's activity expressed in and through my life.

When I was 19 someone commented, "*You have a great ability to preach, but you don't have the Holy Spirit. You need someone to pray for you to receive the Baptism of the Holy Spirit.*" That statement seemed odd, because growing up in a Biblically conservative church, I was under the impression that I already had as much of the Holy Spirit as there was to be had. But soon after that, I allowed a church leader to pray that I would receive this "baptism." As expected, nothing happened – not right away, anyway. However, to my absolute surprise, a few nights later I spontaneously started praying in tongues!

Searching memories of my childhood, I now realize there were many times God tried to break into my earthly reality with supernatural experiences. My theological bias, however, simply did not allow me to believe in or cultivate those types of events. **I was psychologically predisposed to discount spiritual or mystical events**. My earthly reasoning and biased interpretation of the Bible tightly closed the doors on my faith. Yet God kept breaking through those doors of unbelief and doubt, which I disguised as logic and reason.

In my early twenties, I started studying revivals and past moves of God, wondering why we didn't see these phenomena in modern-day America. Reading those accounts revealed a huge void in my heart. While I knew I had experienced momentary touches of God, I dared not go "too far" into the "weird" stuff that I couldn't explain rationally.

While a youth pastor in Baptist churches, God persistently drew closer, even as I stepped back from what I could not understand. At times I would stay up all night praying for a dramatic move of God. In some of those prayer meetings I would literally "feel" a person enter the room. Yet when I looked, I saw no one. I now realize the experience was from God, inviting me into deeper realms.

After studying church growth, my wife and I planted a church according to the latest successful church growth paradigms. We planted a seeker-sensitive Southern Baptist church in a nice neighborhood just outside of Houston, Texas. It was a church that brought people into the knowledge of God slowly and inoffensively by connecting Bible truths with the felt-needs of people. Demonstrations of the Holy Spirit were not considered sensitive to pre-Christians so they were omitted from the church growth strategy. Anything that was considered "seeker-insensitive" according to the latest demographic studies was not included in my corporate plan.

God's persistent mercy found ways to challenge my doubt and unbelief concerning the reality and usefulness of supernatural experiences. During this time, a close friend gave me a copy of Jack Deere's book *Surprised by the Power of the Spirit*. My hungry heart devoured it in one sitting. While I read, the doors of my heart, once barred by doubt and unbelief, swung open and the torrent of longing poured out in my prayers.

While many in our new church followed me as we journeyed into the things of the Spirit, our most sensitive seekers left! Jokingly, I have referred to those days being like Moses in the Exodus of Israel. With my best Charlton Heston voice, I would say, *"Let my people go!"* and out the door they went! As a pastor with a church growth mindset, that really stinks! Even though we really wanted to see miracles, the only "sign and wonder" in those days was that we would put out a "sign" and "wonder" if anyone would show up! Nonetheless – we knew that we were hungry for God, and were willing to do whatever was necessary to experience Him more deeply.

For those who remained, we discovered that, as we welcomed the Lord, it was His good pleasure to give us His Kingdom through glimpses of the supernatural in dreams and visions, physical healings, demonic deliverances, prophetic words and angelic appearances. God's grace and mercy moved in our church with a certain measure of power.

◆ ◆ ◆

After a couple of years, God highlighted Psalm 27:4 as a key for my life. The words "ONE THING I DESIRE" absolutely captured my heart. I began discovering how many other "things" were central to me. The more I meditated, the more my real motives were exposed. Fleshly agendas which had previously fueled desire and passion became brazenly obvious. I was horrified to realize that I wanted God's **activity** more than I wanted **Him**. I sought His blessing on my ambition and masked it in spiritual terminology. Intimacy with God was just too … well, too intimate. God took me through a process of extracting other loves from my life. Whether it was "success" in ministry, church growth or anointing for power, God methodically and lovingly transformed me. He wanted me to be a "one God man."

As a church, we were ushered by the Holy Spirit into months of heart-wrenching intimacy – with one another, in families, among the leadership and within the community. God met us with a gentler form of power – grace for healing the wounds of our hearts. He did this so that we could draw nearer to one another and, ultimately, receive a greater capacity to love Him and receive His love.

My desire to see Him, to know His ways, to be with Him, to experience the full extent of His manifest presence steadily grew. I longed for my spiritual senses to be opened to see what Jesus sees, to hear what Jesus hears and feel what He feels.

One of my problems was the God I read about in the Bible was far greater than the God I was experiencing. I desperately NEEDED to experience and see more of God's activity. So I decided to go where I heard miracles abounded and the faith of people met with the presence of God and healings broke out en masse. I had heard stories of deliverances from demonization and obvious miracles of instant healing. Randy Clark, the man who sparked the Toronto renewal in 1994, had

41

developed a ministry called Global Awakening. He encouraged people to travel with him to places like Brazil where they could experience the power of God beyond their wildest imagination. I desperately wanted to see God move in healings, signs and wonders that defied my previous spiritual realities.

From my very first trip with Randy and Global Awakening, supernatural healings and miracles abounded. The leaders of Global Awakening taught that they could pass on the anointing for supernatural ministry through the laying on of hands. The Bible calls this impartation. Randy and his team prayed for each of us, releasing an impartation to pray for the sick and see miraculous healings. It worked! Many of us entered progressively into gifts of healing and seeing into spiritual realities as a result of their prayers for us. The outpouring of God's love and presence upon the Brazilians was contagious. We not only came under Randy's healing anointing for the mission trip, most of us brought a measure of that anointing home with us.

In Belem, the first city on our ministry trip, hundreds of healings took place, one after another. Many were healed immediately as I laid hands on them. I still carry a photo of a little boy I prayed for named David. God healed him of serious brain damage produced by an oxygen deficiency at birth. As a result of this birth trauma, he couldn't see, because his eyes roamed independently of each other. Nor could he learn to walk because his feet would not flatten out. After praying for him for about an hour, his eyes focused, and his feet straightened! His grandmother's shriek of joy and the contagious smile on his face will be forever embedded in my mind.

The more healings and miracles I saw, the more acutely I felt a deeper hunger stirring in the depths of my being. *I must have more of God*, I thought. Even in the midst of all this supernatural activity, the more power I saw unleashed as crippled legs straightened, blind eyes opened and deaf ears heard, the more I longed for God. *I must have more of God's presence and passion in my life.*

After our series of meetings in Belem, we moved to the next city, Forteleza, where God had a different agenda for me. A verse that I had preached right before leaving my home congregation was out of 1 Corinthians 2:9-10, *"Eye has not seen, nor ear heard, nor have entered into the heart of man the things which God has prepared for those who love Him. But God has revealed them to us by His Spirit. For the Spirit searches all things, yes, the deep things of God."* I prayed that God would give me those "deep things."

In this sermon, I connected this passage from 1 Corinthians 2 with a passage from Daniel 9, which describes the angel Gabriel coming to Daniel while he was seeking understanding. In verse 22, Gabriel said something that reverberated through me: *"O Daniel, I have now come forth to give you skill to understand what you have just seen."*

Pacing in my hotel room, I prayed, *Oh God, I must have the type of revelation that I need angelic help to understand. My current level of revelation is far too shallow. I want the type of revelation that, like Daniel, I cannot understand without angelic help; the type where an angel has to physically manifest from Heaven and give me skill to understand.*

Later that day, at a leader's training, Bill Johnson, pastor of Bethel Church in Redding, California, stood to speak to an overcrowded auditorium. He shared, with much greater authority, the exact same message about revelation of the

43

mysteries of God that I had given in my home congregation. God arrested my attention.

Afterward Bill prayed for me and asked God to give me a spirit of wisdom and revelation. As Bill prayed for me, Gary Oates, the author of *Open My Eyes, Lord*, came and joined in. Gary had a journey similar to mine: From salvation into ministry – plodding along, often in human strength, ministering out of a set of church growth principles and denominational structures, both of us doing the best we could with what we knew. After having a profound encounter, Gary received a gift of impartation that would transfer to others the ability to literally see into the spiritual realm. I asked Gary to pray that my eyes would be opened.

Not long after that, while still in Brazil, I became aware of something in me. For most of my life, unusual things would happen that I would dismiss as my eyes playing tricks on me. Sometimes, I would see orbs of light. Other times, I would see a person with a lighted silhouette of another person appearing right behind them. Oddly, the shadow of light never followed an ordinary or explainable pattern. On this trip, I became aware that this "shadow of light" would follow people as they ministered and would disappear the moment they stopped. At first, I thought my eyes were really tired! But later during that trip, I told Gary about it. He sagely replied that I was beginning to see angels and advised me to cultivate this experience in prayer.

Even after seeing the miracles and becoming aware that I was seeing angels with my natural eyes, I longed to experience more. The increase in the miraculous was clearly evident, but I wanted more of God, Himself.

This led me to take my second trip with Global Awakening – the trip that would revolutionize my life forever. We traveled to Anápolis, Brazil, where Gary and Kathi Oates led the meeting that day. *Little did I know that God would meet me there. It was my time. And, if you are reading these words, it is your time, too.*

As I continue telling the story of how a conservative Baptist preacher started seeing angels, my desire is that it will restore hope that everyone can experience God's tangible presence in the natural realm. My aim is to restore faith that everyone can enter more deeply into His Kingdom, and to encourage you to proactively embrace Kingdom realities. This is who you are. This is what you were designed for. If you have that vague sense of frustration with spiritual mediocrity – If you know you have the destiny of greatness written on your heart but are not yet experiencing it – If you are one of the faithful churchgoers or if you have given up on church altogether – My intention is to rekindle the hope that you can enter into deep encounters with a wild and unpredictable, supernatural God.

The mysteries of His Kingdom are within your reach – so reach! Swing open the doors of the Kingdom and go in like a child. Push past doubt and unbelief and dare to venture into new realms of God's Kingdom. This pursuit was written on your heart by a Creator who longs to be found by you!

Chapter 2
In the Presence of Angels

Are not all angels ministering spirits sent to serve those who will inherit salvation?
Hebrews 1:14

As our bus lurched along the twisting, steep highway between Brasilia and toward the city of Anápolis, I noticed a strange phenomenon in the sky: **a rainbow in a perfect circle around the sun**. I knew that in scripture the rainbow symbolized a covenant promise[1]. But a rainbow around the sun – what could that mean? Please understand, I used to have an aversion to those who would "over spiritualize" events that could otherwise be considered coincidental. Suddenly, the presence of the Lord washed over me. I was meant to pay attention to this sign in the sky. After awhile, God's still, small voice spoke to my heart, declaring a new covenant agreement, whispering that I was entering into an open heaven over my life. Anticipation rose within me. Something was going to happen in this city. Something big. I was about to experience a "suddenly" of God.

So, it began as just a normal Wednesday on a mission trip. That morning, as was our routine, we ate breakfast, left our hotel, boarded the bus and drove the short distance into town. The little church, tucked in among small businesses, storefronts and auto repair shops, looked more like a store than a center for worship. As we entered, the sounds of the highway traffic

---

[1] Genesis 9:12-17

mingled with the chatter of Brazilians excited to see the American healing team on a weekday morning. By the time the first worship chords were struck, the church was packed with more than 300 people, squeezed into all available chairs and floor space, seeking God's presence and power.

A variety of citizens came that day – young and old, men and women. Some came to receive healing for their bodies, longing for more than the temporary alleviation of symptoms offered by the pharmacy down the street. Others came for healing of their hearts, their eyes full of loss and longing. Many came out of curiosity mixed with desire to experience more of God. Their expectations infused the atmosphere with faith. God was tangibly there. He would meet them there. And, though I did not know it at the time, God would meet me there, too.

God is calling people from all across the spectrum of humanity – not just the spiritually elite, not just North Americans, not just special leaders from various nations. God calls the humble and the broken, those in need of a Savior, Healer and Friend. He actively looks for those who are hungry for Him. Scripture tells us that His eyes "run to and fro throughout the whole earth, to show Himself strong on behalf of those whose heart is loyal to Him."[1] God desires people to encounter – perhaps even more than most people want to encounter Him!

God's grace is really amazing. If there was ever someone God had to lavish with grace to even begin to desire these types of experiences – it was me! I used to sit in front of the television and mock the faith healing evangelists. Unlike my

---

[1] 2 Chronicles 16:9

history with the activity of the Holy Spirit, these Brazilians came with an expectant faith, a respectful faith. The patience God extended toward me was astonishing.

Ten years ago if anyone had told me they had seen an angel at church, or expected to see angels anywhere, I would have suggested that **they** should be seen … by a mental health professional! But God's everlasting mercy overtook my doubt and unbelief and I experienced a 180 degree reversal. Now, instead of mocking, I found myself earnestly desiring to experience His supernatural presence and power.

Before going to Brazil, my personal spiritual awakening led me to various prophetic conferences where I would pray, *Oh God, please have the prophet call me out*. I thought the zenith of spiritual encounters was to be called out from a crowd by a prophetic guy who would say something like, "There's a half Asian man named Lucas pastoring a small congregation in Sugar Land, Texas, whose birthday is March 19th. God wants you to know…" Then the prophet would proceed to give profound revelation that would change the course of world history. But, it never happened.

I hoped and was disappointed. Hope deferred made my heart sick with longing. While never confessing it out loud, I began to despair of ever seeing God in the supernatural dimensions. It seemed as if God's Spirit would touch everyone else and just pass me by. I was that desperate. But, God is not the God of our timing. He has timing of His own. On that Wednesday morning in Anápolis, Brazil, He met us all in an extraordinary way.

◆◆◆

I was sitting in the back of the auditorium in Anápolis. The worship swept everyone into the embrace of God. Eventually, sounds of deliverance filled the air as loud cries indicated that deep emotional healings were taking place and that people were being released from demonic oppression. Youth stomped and rocked as the passion of God filled them with holy fire. But I was oblivious to the noise. Unusually, I did not feel that pastoral compulsion to get up and minister.

I was worshipping as I normally do, with my eyes closed. Opening my eyes for just a moment, I saw a sudden flurry of light encompassing me. My natural eyes could see a tornado of swirling lights rushing around the room. "Lord what is this?" I asked.

"Angels," He softly replied. He was allowing my physical eyes to see!

"Wow!" Not a very spiritual response, I know, but it was about all I could say. I prayed for more clarity. Soon, I saw angels all around. In fact, some were swooping down, flying so close to my head that I ducked to avoid being hit.

I looked up toward the stage and there to the left stood a huge, terrible looking man with dark hair. He was fierce and ugly. Soon, Gary Oates took the microphone and said, "There is a warrior angel here," and pointed to the exact same spot where I was looking.

So that's what warrior angels look like! I thought. Others had described them as ugly. The confirmation that I was seeing the same angel as Gary really boosted my faith.

Then, the Lord spoke to me and said, **"Go have Kathi Oates pray for you and I will change your life forever."**

This was problematic for me. Kathi was sitting in the front row with an empty chair next to her, but I was in the back of the auditorium. Gary had not extended an invitation to go forward. He had just started sharing the message on his heart. I wrestled with God over this issue. I did not want to crawl over all the Brazilians that were packed like sardines in rows on my right and left. *Oh please, God, no! I am not going to make a scene and crawl up there, disrupting everyone. They aren't even singing 'Just As I Am' yet!*

In God's kindness, Kathi, for reasons she did not know, got up and moved to the back of the auditorium. She sat close to the side where a seat "just happened" to be open beside her. God is kind even when we argue with Him. *Now, this, I can do,* I reasoned. Sitting down in the empty seat beside her, I explained what was happening and asked her to pray for me. She put her hand on my back, after that, I was no longer aware of her or anyone else in the room.

In fact, if Kathi had told me that I literally disappeared from the room at that moment, it would not have surprised me. Actually, the next earthly memory I have is of several people helping me, shaking and trembling, onto the bus several hours later.

What transpired after Kathi began to pray was not a vision. Nor was it a mental picture. It was real. It was as real as me typing on this computer and as real as you reading these words.

Just after Kathi began praying for me, a beautiful angel walked toward me. Suddenly, whether I was in the body or out of the body, I do not know. The room faded, and I stood silent and alone before a winged angel, dressed in white with gold chain-link armor. As I watched him walk toward me, he didn't say much, but what he said and did has changed me forever. Several hours later, in my hotel room, I recorded the experience in my journal:

I saw the angel of the Lord come toward me with a sword in his right hand. Light flashed from the sword – whether the light emanated from inside the sword or was from some external source – I do not know. The expression on his face was very benevolent, but as he walked toward me it suddenly changed. It was the reluctant look of someone who had to do something they really did not want to do.

He lifted the sword and swiftly and purposefully plunged the blade deep into my heart. As the blade entered my chest cavity to the hilt, I doubled over in pain, feeling it cut into my flesh. The pain was so intense I felt as though I had died. Then the angel's hand began guiding the sword around the circumference of my heart – not just once, but over and over again. I felt as if he was "circumcising" my heart. As the angel circled the sword around and around my heart, I felt years of "stuff" falling off of me. Hurts and strongholds were gone in an instant. Along with the pain, I felt the weight of years sloughing off. I can still feel the effects in my physical heart even now, as I write this.

The angel took a step back. It was then I noticed he had another instrument in his left hand. It looked like some kind of lamp, but he used it as a flame thrower. The angel began directing fire toward me. He began to shoot fire onto my feet and said he was lighting my feet on fire to run to the

51

nations. As the flames touched my feet in this supernatural experience, my feet in the natural got uncomfortably hot. Right now (3 o'clock in the afternoon, Brazil time – the meeting was this morning) my feet are still on fire.

The angel began to move to other parts of my body lighting them on fire. The room was nice and cool, yet I was sweating profusely. The angel directed the flame thrower toward my hands. He said, "I'm lighting your hands on fire to bring healing to the masses." Then, he directed flames toward my eyes and said, "I'm preparing your eyes to see the beauty of the King." He also said, "Gone are the days when just doing what you know to do will suffice." He said that I would be able to see and know precisely what steps I was to take. He also told me that what I saw I would need to obey immediately. As my emotions surfaced, a wave of unworthiness hit me, but I wanted to receive all the angel was saying and doing.

Then the angel asked me if I wanted to see the King. Though I said yes, I was surprised at the reluctance that was mixed with the excitement in my response. He then showed me the Lord. I cannot describe how beautiful, how terrible, and how amazing Jesus looked. He had jet black hair and very dramatic features, but His eyes were what amazed me most. I cannot accurately describe them with words. They were piercing yet gentle at the same time. They were intense but meek. They were filled with passion. I could tell there was absolutely no compromise in those eyes, yet they were the eyes of the most gracious and good man I had ever met.

Despite His striking appearance, what affected me the most was the fact that I didn't recognize Him. I saw the

Lord – and He wasn't a "familiar face" to me. His was the face of a stranger. He didn't look like I thought He was going to look. I wept and am still weeping as I write this. I am stirred with great conviction over the fact that I did not recognize Him – but there is an even deeper stirring of hunger to get to know Him.

Suddenly, before my eyes, Jesus began to transform into a lion. It was the most majestic, regal and magnificent lion I have ever seen. He was sitting composed and confident, looking over His creation. His eyes seemed to see everything. His chest was very broad and His mane was flowing in the wind. As I watched, the lion opened its mouth to roar, but I heard no sound. Though I saw it rather than heard it, this roar shook me for hours afterwards. It felt as if the molecules in my body were being rearranged.

Then he asked me if I wanted to see what the Lord was doing in Anápolis. I said yes. He gave me a wide-angle, aerial view of the city of Anápolis. Suspended above it was a giant ball of fire. It was the fire of revival and a giant move of His Spirit ready to be released, yet still hanging above the city in a giant net. The giant orb strained to break through the net, but was constrained by the crisscrossed ropes. Every once in a while a fragment of the fireball would drop through the net and touch people. At times bigger pieces of fire would fall – but the enormous bulging mass of fire was still hanging suspended, prevented from falling by the net that restrained it.

Then the angel asked me if I wanted to see the net that was stopping the ball of fire from falling. I said yes. He brought me close enough to see the net. The crisscrossed cables that composed the net had two different phrases written on them – UNFORGIVENESS AND BROKEN RELATIONSHIPS. In other words, if unforgiveness and broken relationships were not there, there would be no net restraining the Spirit's fire from falling in Anápolis.

Then, suddenly the encounter ended. I was collected from the floor and loaded onto the shuttle back to my hotel room. As soon as I was able, I pulled out my journal and began recording what had just occurred. I was "buzzing" inside, still feeling the aftershock as I began to write.

God released many profound mysteries to me during this encounter. As I continue to ponder the meaning of all that I experienced, I am discovering that this encounter was for the entire Body of Christ as much as it was for me. It is for your city as much as it is for Anápolis, Brazil. The mysteries that were revealed in those few minutes in that little church have huge implications for the Body of Christ. **It is true: this was meant for you just as much as it was for me.**

While that day started as a normal day on a mission trip, suddenly everything changed. God did not ease me into the encounter. It happened in a moment. It happened quickly. My life was totally transformed, and at the same time, my life was opened up to an exciting new process of transformation that continues today. But this transformation was not only for me, it is for everyone who will receive it. Many have encountered God in such ways, and they are now moving so rapidly they wonder if they can handle it. The deeper realms of God are open for all who want access. The invitation has been offered. Now the choice is simply ours to make. This could very well be your moment.

Chapter 3
Matters of the Heart

*Praise the Lord, you his angels, You mighty ones who do his
bidding, Who obey his words.*
Psalm 103:20

I saw the angel of the Lord come toward me with a
sword in his right hand. Light flashed from the sword –
whether the light emanated from inside the sword or was
from some external source – I do not know. The expression
on his face was very benevolent, but as he walked toward me
it suddenly changed. It was the reluctant look of someone
who had to do something they really did not want to do.

He lifted the sword and swiftly and purposefully
plunged the blade deep into my heart. As the blade entered
my chest cavity to the hilt, I doubled over in pain, feeling it
cut into my flesh. The pain was so intense I felt as though I
had died. Then the angel's hand began guiding the sword
around the circumference of my heart – not just once, but
over and over again. I felt as if he was "circumcising" my
heart. As the angel circled the sword around and around my
heart, I felt years of "stuff" falling off of me. Hurts and
strongholds were gone in an instant. Along with the pain, I
felt the weight of years sloughing off. I can still feel the
effects in my physical heart even now, as I write this.

God is ready and eager to take us to higher levels of
interaction with supernatural realities. He stands poised to launch
us into seasons of acceleration. Likewise, God is ready and eager

to take us to deeper levels of healing and personal freedom that could otherwise restrict the depth of revelation God is waiting to give us. When the Lord comes and cuts away all that hinders us, we can run victoriously the race that is set before us.

The sword that pierced me that day symbolized the Word of God. Hebrews 4:12 states, "the Word of God is living and powerful, and sharper than any two-edged sword, piercing even to the division of soul and spirit, and of joints and marrow, and is a discerner of the thoughts and intents of the heart." In the right hands, the sword becomes a surgeon's scalpel that carves through flesh, discerns the motives and intents of the heart, and cuts away the sins that so easily beset us, releasing us from the "baggage of the past."

This is actually the second time I experienced a sword piercing me. Repetition is a powerful teacher, but when swords are involved it really hurts! The first time, at the Toronto Airport Christian Fellowship, Carol Arnott gave a call for individuals who wanted an impartation of the sword of the Lord. Back then, I interpreted the sword as an offensive weapon that would assist me in ministry, so I went forward to receive it through impartation. As Carol prayed for me, she said, "You will not wield this sword – it will wield you." As she prayed, I fell down and began having a vision. Overwhelmed by the power of the Holy Spirit, I reached out and grabbed the sword. It wobbled all over the place for several moments, then suddenly turned and plunged into my chest! The Word of God pierced my heart that day.

This time in Brazil, the angel wielded the sword and drove it deep into my chest. He did not remove it, but carefully and purposefully guided the sword in a circular motion repeatedly around my heart. Oddly, I could actually hear the sound of it ripping through the muscles, bones and tendons of my chest cavity. I not only heard it but felt it circling, cutting around my heart; the excruciating pain searing my entire being. I couldn't stand it. No anesthesia, no comforting words, just this ruthless sword repeating its circular motion, rending and slicing my chest cavity, making me feel as though it was literally killing me.

The angel went about his job with calculated determination etched on his face. He did not ask my permission, though there was a fundamental 'yes' in my heart. There was no attempt on my part to hold back anything from the painful incision as the sword went around and around. Nor did it occur to me, to say, *"Yeah, you can cut this, but don't cut that."* The whole point was for him to get it over with and finally finish!

Despite the pain, I began to feel a heaviness falling off my soul. My shoulders straightened as years of painful issues sloughed away, along with my false pretenses of pride, anger, rejection, control, shame and fear as the angel circled the sword around and around for what seemed like an eternity.

I don't remember the angel ever pulling the sword out. In fact, I can still feel the sting of it at certain times even now. Whether in a worship service or when someone is praying for me, there are moments when I still feel it quite distinctly.

When I shared my experience with Randy Clark, he described to me some historical accounts of people with precisely the same spiritual experience. When those saints died, autopsies revealed scar tissue around their hearts. The experience I had was so real and so painful that it would not surprise me if there are physical marks where the sword had carved its way around my heart.

Kathi Oates, upon hearing this part of the encounter, suggested that God was circumcising my heart. Colossians 2:11 says, "In Him you were also circumcised with the circumcision made without hands, by putting off the body of the sins of the flesh, by the circumcision of Christ." The Lord is cutting away all excess weight and encumbrance that hinders us from coming into our full destiny. He brings us into deeper levels of healing so that we will be able to see more clearly into the spiritual realm. But, paradoxically, He allows us to see and experience more in order to bring us into deeper levels of healing. God is circumcising our hearts. We cannot get where God is taking us without going through a radical circumcision of the heart.

God can do in an instant what it takes us months of ministry and counseling to accomplish. God wants His children to be free and act as free people! Please do not misunderstand. I am still in a growth process with God. But, as a result of this circumcision of the heart, this growth process has simply sped up and intensified.

Legalized slavery was one of the great atrocities of American history. The thought of one person owning another in today's world is repulsive. It is repugnant to think that any person created in God's image would be reduced to a piece of property. But it is similarly repugnant for Christians to live as slaves when they are absolutely free.

58

For much of my life, I was a slave to certain weights on my soul. Some of these were outright sin habits. Other weights were strongholds, deeply engrained ungodly belief patterns. There were even weights in my life that appeared to be good things. They were weights, because they did not fuel my passion for Jesus. It was like running with ankle weights strapped to my legs. I could run, but not in the fullness of God's desire.

Many Christians have similar feelings. Spiritually, it seems as though they are walking in quicksand. They take one step forward, and sink an inch. They desperately want more of God and His Kingdom in their lives, but often find themselves stumbling, or even falling. The pattern of sinning and confessing, walking and falling, becomes a vicious cycle. When we settle for this mediocrity, we are enslaved.

Something happens when the Spirit begins to move. It becomes increasingly difficult for people to maintain the status quo. In other words it becomes virtually impossible to dictate what we will, or will not, allow God to do. When the Holy Spirit moves, it is difficult to remain in homeostasis. The Holy Spirit and sin will not coexist. Either the Holy Spirit will expose sin or sin will quench the Spirit. There is no middle ground. The Holy Spirit begins cleaning house.

Interestingly enough, many times, the first response when the issues of our hearts are exposed is to hide. We follow after the pattern exhibited first in Adam and Eve: we try to cover up!

When our church began to discover how God can set people radically free, we offered personal ministry to that end.

Oddly, many Christians were extremely reluctant to avail themselves of this ministry. They resisted taking the simple steps necessary for walking in more complete victory, preferring to remain in their own measure of comfort rather than risk entering into the full manifestation of their salvation, healing and deliverance. We frequently found that those who appeared to be most uncomfortable with receiving ministry exhibited the greatest symptoms and indicators that something lurked on the other side of that door to freedom – something that wanted them stuck in one place forever. This was especially true for those who had been around church the longest. Perhaps fear, anxiety, spiritual pride and a host of other issues were at the heart of their reluctance. Yet great freedom awaited those who pressed beyond those issues.

A deception that poses one of the most serious obstacles to receiving ministry is this: we do not realize how full of glory we really are! Some struggled to receive prayer ministry, because they do not want to be God's "fixer-upper project." Their paradigm is that God is looking for their sin and shame instead of looking for their glory and gold. If we believe God is looking for what is wrong, then we will view such ministry as "tinkering" and "fixing." If we believe God is looking for what is right, then we will welcome such ministry as a powerful tool for removing that which obscures our beauty in God. If God's goal is for us to focus on our sin and emotional hurts, it would lead to a lifestyle of an unhealthy introspection, which is not godly. God's goal is for us to focus on Him and His beauty as it is revealed to us and through us.

When true freedom comes, hindrances in our lives are healed as we fix our eyes upon the Lord. As we gaze upon the Lord, we do not move from being sinners to saints. That happened at salvation. After salvation, we move from "glory to glory." We move from good to better. We are full of glory! Our journey is from holy to more holy. This paradigm shift empowers us to enthusiastically embrace ministry that heals the heart. God is not trying to fix up an old piece of junk – He is changing us from one level of glory to another. The main issue is not that something is "so wrong" with us. Rather the issue is that something is "so right" with us. The goal, then, becomes to remove everything that hinders our glory from becoming more radiantly and measurably manifest.

If you find yourself becoming increasingly uncomfortable as you read this, it may be a good sign. The Spirit of God is doing something in your heart. It has been well stated by Bill Johnson, *"If we're already comfortable, what need do we have for the Comforter?"*

The second, no less powerful reason we sometimes resist receiving prayer ministry is the issue of trust. I personally discovered that God is more concerned with our freedom than with coddling our lack of trust. The Holy Spirit is very intentional about this. Paul says this, "Work out your own salvation with fear and trembling."[1] The Greek word that we translate "saved" actually encompasses salvation, healing and deliverance. Paul is saying, work out your salvation, healing and deliverance to its end result. Work it to its final conclusion, which is pure sanctification. We are commanded to work out our salvation until nothing hinders us, nothing makes us afraid, and nothing controls us – until we don't have to manage our image,

---

[1] Philippians 2:12

until we are not worried about what others think, **until we are just free**. Work out your salvation to its end result.

God will not work out your salvation for you. He commanded you to do it! You work it out by agreeing and partnering with God. Your agreement sounds something like, *God, I do not want <u>anything</u> to hinder the life of Christ being fully formed in me. I choose to think differently – repent. I am free so help me act free – and remove anything that hinders my freedom. Set me free to live abundantly the life You have given me.*

We all have "blind spots," areas of our lives where we need healing that we are usually not able to identify without the help of trusted friends. In order to rise to higher levels of supernatural realities, God must address our blind spots. It takes a loving and trustworthy community of brothers and sisters to gracefully point them out and bring healing. The New Testament says that if we live in meaningful transparency, when we pray for one another, we will be healed.[1] Our blind spots hinder us from seeing in the Spirit. Growing in the awareness of our blind spots takes time, much work and a loving spiritual family that is committed to our freedom.

Concerning my experience with the angel's sword, perhaps God was giving me a foretaste of what is to come with inner healing en masse. My sense is that this experience contains potential that was for more than my personal healing.

In the past, people prayed for weeks and months to break into the assurance of salvation. Historical accounts of the First

---

[1] James 5:16

and Second Great Awakenings speak of people praying for extended seasons for "breakthrough." They roped off special sections in their meeting places for "inquirers," those who were seeking salvation. There, they would pray, beg and travail until they finally apprehended a personal revelation that Jesus had indeed cleansed them of their sins and come to dwell in their hearts.

To us, that sounds a little absurd. But for many years we have stood for, taught and eventually established that salvation is an act of faith by grace, so now we are able to teach and expect salvation to be received in a moment. We have contended that salvation is not a drawn out process but can happen in an instant. Consequently, today we simply pray, *Lord Jesus, cleanse my sins and come live in my heart,* and He does. Do you remember the moment you got saved? You asked Him, He did it and you felt it that very moment! We are partaking of the inheritance for which believers in previous decades fought. The zenith of their experience has become routine for us.

Right now, what we know as inner healing, deliverance and freedom takes time, and in many cases, repeated prayer – much like the salvation experience in the seventeenth and eighteenth centuries. In the future, though, the sanctification and inner healing for which we persevere could be instantaneous and immediate. We would receive it by faith in a moment just for the asking, like salvation. Then, we would simply pray, *Jesus, set me free*, and His tangible presence, ever increasing in our midst, would meet our faith and ensure dramatic results. God would circumcise our hearts instantly. The fruit of our lives would prove that the Lord set us free in a moment. **That is something worth contending for during this present move of God.**

I see the potential of a generation of leaders teaching, with an assurance of faith, immediate healing of the heart from a good, loving and gracious God who longs to give His children the fullness of salvation, deliverance and healing.

Perhaps one day, the angel's sword will pierce our hearts en masse in widespread and dramatic displays of God's sanctifying power, and all that hinders us will fall away. We must commit ourselves to not allow anything to hinder us. Perhaps the future is now, and all you need to do is pray, *Jesus, set me free.*

Until that day of instantaneous sanctification, freedom from our issues, hurts and ungodly patterns must be pursued. God did instruct us to work out our own salvation which means He will not do it for us. So what can we do to this end?

First, make your focus the Lord Jesus. Many times I have witnessed people allowing their various issues to become the central focus of their lives. How tragic this is! Problems are never fixed when problems are the focus. Problems in our lives are fixed only when the solutions are our focus. At the risk of sounding over-simplistic, Jesus really is the solution to every problem so He should be the focus!

With Him as our focus, we can then practically engage in activities, habits, and practices that open the doors to our personal freedom. Prayer ministry, deliverance ministry, spiritual counseling, accountable relationships are all very wise steps we can take on the road to establishing personal freedom. Involvement with a local community of believers is an absolute must. God is raising up a wide spectrum of ministries and resources in this hour that help Christians live in freedom. Many inner healing and deliverance ministries are quite effective. Avail yourself to every resource God has provided.

Jesus purchased your freedom on the cross. Now it's your right and privilege to live it! Be free!

Chapter 4
The Fire of God

He makes his angels winds, His servants flames of fire.
Hebrews 1:7

The angel took a step back. It was then I noticed he had another instrument in his left hand. It looked like some kind of lamp, but he used it as a flame thrower. The angel began directing fire toward me. He began to shoot fire onto my feet and said he was lighting my feet on fire to run to the nations. As the flames touched my feet in this supernatural experience, my feet in the natural got uncomfortably hot. Right now (3 o'clock in the afternoon, Brazil time – the meeting was this morning) my feet are still on fire.

The angel began to move to other parts of my body lighting them on fire. The room was nice and cool, yet I was sweating profusely. The angel directed the flame thrower toward my hands. He said, "I'm lighting your hands on fire to bring healing to the masses." Then, he directed flames toward my eyes and said, "I'm preparing your eyes to see the beauty of the King." He also said, "Gone are the days when just doing what you know to do will suffice." He said that I would be able to see and know precisely what steps I was to take. He also told me that what I saw I would need to obey immediately. As my emotions surfaced, a wave of unworthiness hit me, but I wanted to receive all the angel was saying and doing.

For a long time, I thought God's fire could only represent His judgment. Thoughts of Sodom and Gomorrah and

66

hell would flood my mind. But I now see that, when God's passion burns for his children, fire also represents His intense affection. If we view God as angry and impersonal, we tend to see fire as the flaring temper of a detached and hard-to-please father. God is not like that. He is full of emotions – good ones, too!

"God is love."[1] He is synonymous with love. His intense love burns with zealous affection for me, for you, for your family, your neighbors, your co-workers and your friends. He invites us to share in the passions of His heart – justice for the poor, healing for the nations, and in the immense love He has for all humanity. He is good!

Simply stated, fire is God's passion about any subject. This new perspective helped me make sense of this experience: an angel with a flamethrower – aimed at me!

The angel held the flame thrower, and with great care and purpose, directed it at me. Then, ***Whoosh,*** FIRE! By the time this segment of the encounter was finished, I was totally immersed in flame and completely overwhelmed by the intensity of God's love for me. As I was saturated with divine passion, I began to understand that there is no apathy in God whatsoever. There is no status quo. There is no ho-hum. His affection burns like a "most vehement flame."[2] It is not the half-hearted fondness of a disinterested, distracted father. It is intentional, direct, purposeful, and HOT.

---

[1] 1 John 4:8
[2] Song of Solomon 8:6

67

From the moment the angel blasted me with the flamethrower, my body began radiating heat and large drops of sweat were rolling off my forehead, down my back and arms, sticking my shirt to my body. Kathi Oates, though I did not know it at the time, still had her hand on my back, confirmed this as we remembered the experience later that night. She said that as she was praying for me, there was a point when I started radiating heat. Even at 5:30 that afternoon, when I went to Randy Clark's hotel room to tell him about the experience, he could feel heat emanating from my body. He said that when I approached him, he was surprised by the intensity of the power and heat.

As the angel was immersing me in flame, he made statements focused on three areas: my feet, my hands and my eyes. As I have shared these statements in conferences and other meetings, other people have entered into the same type of manifestation in their bodies. My experience becomes their experience. As you read, it could become yours as well.

When he immersed my feet in flames, he said, "I am lighting your feet on fire to run to the nations."

The feet are the foundation of the body. God speaks of His Son's dominion by declaring all things to be under His feet. Ephesians 1:22 says, "…and he [God] put all things in subjection under his [Jesus'] feet …" Similarly, our feet symbolize our dominion, ownership and lordship over whatever we are standing on.

Ephesians 1:22 goes on to say that God "gave Jesus to be head over all things to the Church, which is His body…" If all things are in subjection under Jesus' feet, and if we are His body, then it follows that our feet, when dedicated to God's purpose, become the agent of His dominion. The foundation of the body, our feet, are meant to RUN! I can think of few things worse than standing still when you have hot feet!

Christians have a mission of utmost importance. The nations, our neighbors, all of humanity will not come to us – we must go to them! Our impact on the planet is destined to be so much more than sending out a couple of missionaries and handing out a few tracts. Having my feet set ablaze was a precursor to the new mindset that is taking hold in the Church today: one that is prepared to **go** instead of expecting others to **come**. Pre-Christians were never commanded to come to us – we were commanded to go to them, armed with the love of God and not with religious arguments. Whether it's to Africa, Brazil, our neighbors, our co-workers or the homeless shelter downtown, we are commissioned to go and impact the world. This is about more than "soul winning" or sharing a memorized presentation, it is about infiltrating our societies with the culture of the Kingdom of God.

God calls us to develop very intentional, proactive lifestyles resulting in us being a blessing to all people, Christians and pre-Christians alike. God's goodness and kindness lead people to repent.[1] It is imperative that we "re-present" God's goodness so that others can see a living demonstration of His character. People are crying out night and day for apostolic power to be poured out in their communities. Many ask the Lord to move, and now God is asking **us** to move! We are the body of Christ, meant to move as the answer to those prayers! Fire drives our feet to move, love compels us to go.

---

[1] Romans 2:4

When he directed fire onto my hands, he said, "I'm lighting your hands on fire to bring healing to the masses."

I watched the flamethrower travel up from my feet to my hands. Instantly my hands were enveloped in flames. Scripture is replete with examples of hands symbolizing the activity of God. Outstretched hands bless;[1] redeem;[2] release miracles of nature;[3] send people out to battle;[4] reach out to God in intercession;[5] rescue and deliver;[6]; assist the poor;[7] heal the lepers;[8] save the drowning;[9] and heal and release signs and wonders that testify of the presence and power of God.[10]

My journey into divine healing has had its ups and downs. I have prayed for the sick regularly, but there were times I did so as an act of pure obedience rather than because of the very low success rate! There were even times that, when I prayed for the sick, some would actually get sicker!

But when healings do happen…wow! It is indescribable to watch a formerly blind person see for the first time or feel a tumor disappear beneath your hand. I can personally testify that God is still doing this! But please do not believe that healing ministry is the exclusive right of a few high profile Christians. All Christians have been authorized to pray for the sick and to stand in faith for results.

---

[1] Genesis 48:14
[2] Exodus 6:6
[3] Exodus 7 & 14
[4] Joshua 8:19
[5] Psalm 77:2
[6] Psalm 144:7
[7] Proverbs 31:20
[8] Matthew 8:3
[9] Matthew 14:31
[10] Acts 4:30

Most of those in need of healing are not attending a church service on any given Sunday. The reason for this is obvious – they are sick! People who are sick do not usually go to church, at least not yet! So we must take healing to them. If the only time healings and miracles work is in the friendly context of a church service or crusade, we have entirely missed the point. Jesus has commissioned us to stretch forth our hands to heal the sick, cleanse lepers, and raise the dead.[1] Unless we selectively apply the Bible, this command is for all followers of Jesus. Healings can and should happen everywhere: your local store, the lunchroom at your school or work, the gas station, or wherever. The fire compels us to stretch out our hands in blessing everywhere we go.

When he directed flames toward my eyes, he said, "I'm preparing your eyes to see the beauty of the King."

The angel moved from my feet to my hands and then to my eyes, immersing each in turn with fire. It is commonly said that the eyes are the windows of the soul. Whatever the condition of the soul, whether hate or anger, love or peace, it is all telegraphed through the eyes. If eyes are windows of the human soul, how much more are they the windows of the Lord's soul!

The eyes communicate the internal condition of the soul to the outside world. But, they are also windows from the external world inward. Whatever your eyes see enters your being and, to some degree, leaves an impression to which you conform. This is the principle of beholding and becoming; we become what we behold. The Apostle Paul put it this way: *"But we all, with unveiled face, beholding as in a mirror the glory of*

---

[1] Matthew 10:8

71

the Lord, are being transformed into the same image from glory to glory, just as by the Spirit of the Lord."[1]

As my eyes were seared by the intense heat of this fire, the temptation to be fascinated with anything less than the face of God suddenly grew weaker. I now understand how God could want His Bride, the Church, to have eyes only for Him!

I have seen angels with my natural eyes. Angelic ministry is astounding. It is amazing to witness these fiery beings carrying out the commands of the Lord.[2] Many of them are very beautiful, while others look fierce and menacing. But, in all honesty, once you have seen the King, Himself, angels, even the most beautiful ones, pale in comparison. Nothing compares to seeing Him. **Absolutely nothing**.

Many people are being healed in our services. I want more of that, too. My thankful prayer is constantly, *More, Lord.* But if He isn't our divine obsession, we have tragically missed the point. The goal of all our seeking and pursuing is: His face, His beauty, His presence.

There is a very real temptation to be distracted by what God is doing. God never calls us primarily to "Wow" us with what He does. Rather, His goal for us is to walk in greater intimacy with Him. Out of that place of intimacy, great things can and do occur. In the middle of God amazing us, we must have eyes only for Him. There are people with incredible healing gifts and worldwide ministries. Tragically some have lost their focus, and turned their gaze from the King and have begun to fixate on other things.

---

[1] 2 Corinthians 3:18
[2] Psalm 103:20

72

God is preparing us to see the King in His beauty. He repeatedly says to seek His face. Are you ready to see Him? Are you ready for God to get you ready?

The next thing the angel said was, "Gone are the days when just doing what you know to do will suffice."

Our church has journeyed from being a seeker-sensitive Baptist church, into a realm of the supernatural that we never dreamed of or anticipated. Early in our journey, the Holy Spirit wrecked all our church's strategic plans. After my well-designed church growth blueprint was reduced to rubble, I went through a bit of a crisis. Without church growth formulas and programming, I found myself not knowing how to lead. I was constantly second-guessing myself, and, at first, lacked the confidence needed to lead a congregation through such an incredible journey. During that season of our journey I frequently said things like, "I don't know what we're doing," and "I don't know where we're going." While I was attempting to convey that I was yielding to the leadership of the Holy Spirit, I was telegraphing my woeful lack of confidence.

The words that the angel spoke to me in no uncertain terms were later confirmed by Kathi Oates who repeated them almost verbatim. She also told me that God was giving me "laser vision," and that I would know exactly what steps to take. These words brought about a very enthusiastic repentance for saying such things.

While it is true that God never changes who He is, it is also true that He rarely does things the same way twice. You will always know where you stand with God, but you will rarely know what He is going to do next. For leaders coming out of a

73

system of religious control, the initial adjustment can result in a lack of confidence. The culture of Heaven is so different from the culture of religion that it can produce fear and instability for those trying to lead a congregation through the transition. At some points along the journey all we know is, as long as we hold His hand, we will be alright.

So intense and deliberate was the angel's message, I now know that God wants to give us more than an optimistic, "Onward through the fog!" leadership style. He does not want us constantly second guessing our decisions and putting ourselves down. He said that His Word would be a lamp to my feet.[1] He said that He has placed my feet upon a rock.[2] He also emphatically promised that my feet would not slip.[3] God's plan for our lives is not hidden **from** us – it is hidden **for** us to discover. Perhaps His plan is not yet revealed, but we can be confident until more clarity comes. God wants us to walk with boldness into the deeper places with confidence.

God is giving us eyes to see where we are going. He is giving us wisdom to know what we're doing, and He is giving it to us collectively. He is not giving the entire revelation to any one individual. Since there is much revelation given to many people, it will be necessary to receive input from others. He is releasing laser vision for us to see exactly where we need to go and wisdom and strategies to know exactly what we need to do. The spirit of wisdom and revelation is held collectively. We don't want the revelation without wisdom, nor the wisdom

---

[1] Psalm 119:105
[2] Psalm 40:2
[3] Psalm 121:3

without the revelation. We are living in an hour of human history where we need both.

John's announcement about Jesus in Matthew 3:11 was that Jesus would baptize us, not only with the Holy Spirit, but also with fire. Perhaps you have received the baptism of the Holy Spirit. You may speak in tongues, pray for the sick, cast out demons and disciple others. But now, will you receive the baptism of fire? God is doing this in many places right now!

As a result of relating my experience with the fire of God, others have had similar experiences.

After this experience in Anápolis, the next city on our mission was Imperatriz. There, I told the story of my encounter with the angel. As I was speaking, I saw the flamethrower angel come into the auditorium where we were meeting. Because of that, I knew that I could invite people forward who wanted a fresh touch of fire. When I gave the invitation, a stampede ensued – neither protocol, nor dignity held them back. The pastor of the church in Imperatriz stood astonished at the response of his congregation. He slumped over the pulpit and sobbed as members of his congregation cried out for fire. A collective roar arose, *"If you've got fire, and you can release it, then I want it!"* People started feeling fire in the same way I did. That night, the Lord was also present to heal several blind and deaf people.

When I returned to the States, Randy invited me to share this experience at a conference in Harrisburg, Pennsylvania. As I spoke, people later testified that their eyes, hands, and feet were burning. Many later told me of spiritual experiences and

75

profound encounters with angels. The most powerful testimonies were from people who just felt God had given them access into deeper places of intimacy.

Even as you read this, some of you are feeling heat in your eyes. Others are feeling heat in your hands. Still others are feeling the flames starting to engulf their feet. Do not write that off as coincidence. This experience is easily transmittable. God is releasing it to you just as He did to me. It happens nearly every time I share this story. Receive what the Lord is doing right now as you read.

As a result of my eyes being purified by fire, I am a part of an ever increasing company of Christians who are beginning to see angelic activity with much more clarity and frequency. We are fighting for a culture where people regularly see the Lord, where angelic activity is abundant and seen with the natural eye, and where supernatural signs and wonders testify of heaven breaking into earth. His fire is drawing us into deeper realms of intimacy.

Will you receive that? Ask the Lord to baptize you in His fire. Go wherever you hear of the Lord doing this. If you begin to feel the fire of God, do not easily write it off as coincidental but ask God what He is doing. Ask Him for more! Allow the all-consuming fire of God to consume all of you.

Chapter 5
Do You Want to See the King?

How can I, your servant, talk with you, my Lord? My strength is gone and I can hardly breathe.
Daniel 10:17

Then the angel asked me if I wanted to see the King. Though I said yes, I was surprised at the reluctance that was mixed with the excitement in my response. He then showed me the Lord. I cannot describe how beautiful, how terrible, and how amazing Jesus looked. He had jet black hair and very dramatic features, but His eyes were what amazed me most. I cannot accurately describe them with words. They were piercing yet gentle at the same time. They were intense but meek. They were filled with passion. I could tell there was absolutely no compromise in those eyes, yet they were the eyes of the most gracious and good man I had ever met.

Despite His striking appearance, what affected me the most was the fact that I didn't recognize Him. I saw the Lord – and He wasn't a "familiar face" to me. His was the face of a stranger. He didn't look like I thought He was going to look. I wept and am still weeping as I write this. I am stirred with great conviction over the fact that I did not recognize Him – but there is an even deeper stirring of hunger to get to know Him.

The more I have reflected on this portion of the encounter, the more amazed and completely perplexed I am. This is at the same time the most exhilarating and most convicting part for me. This was the fulfillment of my life's goal – to see the Lord – and yet it was the most disconcerting part of the experience.

As I shared earlier, my only vocational ambition was ministry. I became a Christian when I was nine years old, and began preaching at age sixteen. During high school, I carried my Bible on top of my other books everyday. I started prayer meetings on our school campus. I loved God with all my heart. My dad made me memorize large portions of scripture. If I did not memorize my weekly passage, I would not be allowed to watch cartoons on Saturday. Quite candidly, I liked Scooby-Doo more than I liked memorizing scripture, so I did it, and am thankful for it! I attended a Bible institute right out of high school and during college I became a full time youth pastor. I have been in vocational ministry for most of my adult life. I loved prayer and worship and had a lot of confidence in my knowledge of God.

When the angel asked me, "Do you want to see the King?" my reply was, **"Yes!"** This was, and remains, my greatest desire – to see His face. However, there was also a sense of great hesitancy. Did I *really* want to have a face to face meeting with the King?

Then, it happened: I was standing before the Lord. As we stood together, the reality of the "I AM" registered very deeply within me. He is absolutely indescribable. Words are far too weak a vehicle to communicate my wonder and awe. To accurately describe Him, given the limitations of language, would be a miracle in itself. As powerful as words are, they cannot explain the fullness of God's beauty. Even now as I bring that scene to my mind, it still has the power to undo me.

I had never seen a face so radiant and well-proportioned, features so lovely, hair so vibrantly healthy and alive, yet the feature that riveted my attention the most was His eyes. Those eyes – just one look instantly resolved many of the issues of my heart. They were the eyes of the most genuinely kind person anyone will ever meet, and yet there was a fierce hatred for injustice. He is quite deliberate in all His ways. I knew He could be trusted. No matter what the subject, I knew that, when He speaks, He means it. He loves me, and He likes me. As much as I love His presence, He really loves mine. I know this now, because His eyes communicated all of it instantly, in one glance.

But in His presence, I was deeply convicted by a sobering fact. While I knew this was the Lord, **I realized that I was looking into the face of a perfect stranger**. Tears welled up and began to flow freely. I was astonished and greatly humbled. I prayed, *God, I've sought You most of my life. I have served you in many ways. I have led many people to You. I have spent days in fasting and prayer. All this I have done for You, and I still don't know You as You really are.* I was devastated. However, it created in me a tremendous hunger to know Him more intimately.

If someone had told me that I would not recognize the Lord when I saw Him, I would have quickly dismissed it. Surely, I would recognize Him. After all, I had been in vocational ministry most of my adult life. I wanted intimacy more than anything. He is the "One Thing"[1] of my life, my Magnificent

---

[1] Psalm 27:4

Obsession, whom I pursue above all else. Yet the sobering truth was that He was unfamiliar to me. It has once been said that we are way too familiar with a God we barely know. If this is true it is because it would be far too uncomfortable to really get to know God as He really is.

◆◆◆

In the beginning, God created humans in His own image. The original temptation was that, if Eve ate the fruit of the tree of the knowledge of good and evil, she would become like God.[1] Even though Adam and Eve were already created in the image of God, they forgot who they were, yielded to the pressure of the Evil One, and ate the fruit. Since Adam and Eve succumbed to that temptation, we have tried to make God in our image. Thus, our image of God is infinitely too small.

This is, in part, why many today have distorted feelings toward God. It is because they have "created" Him in equally incorrect ways. This is also how Israel could pray for the coming of the Messiah while Jesus was riding on a donkey just a few feet away.

God is breaking our **images** of who He is to reveal who He **really** is! This is surprising people, and God loves surprises! He is wonderfully unpredictable. I once heard somebody advertise a seminar entitled, *How to Contain the Power of God.* If you can contain it or harness it, it is not God. He is wild beyond human ability to contain. Because of this, as we say *yes*

---

[1] Genesis 2:17, 3:5

to closer intimacy with God, we are going to repeatedly face feelings of discomfort. The revelation of His character will constantly challenge our humanity. As we get to know Him, we are going to be very, very discombobulated.

We tend to have a hard time with a God who likes to constantly change how He works. Most, if not all, of us resist change, especially change that we do not initiate. And absolutely no one likes imposed change. When change is sudden, we would rather think about it and slowly process it before accepting it. God is about to impose many dramatic changes on us. When He does, it will come down to a question of who is really Lord. Who is really King? Do we **really** want to see the King?

God never wants us to depend on what He **does**; instead, He invites us to believe who He **is** and what He is currently saying. Our relationship with God should be such that we cannot follow in the steps of another. We cannot afford to be pressed into the mold of another ministry. God wants all preconceived ideas of Him held loosely. New depths, new mysteries, new secrets of His infinite character are being revealed. His activity is always a reflection of His nature. What a wonderful time to be alive!

The humbling revelation that I did not know Him as I thought did not lead me to shame and condemnation. Rather, it fueled an already existing desire to seek His face. In my heart I thought, *Dear Lord Jesus, I don't know You as I desire, and I will do anything to change that. I must know You.*

Though the Lord Jesus was physically manifest before me, this was by no means the fullness of the revelation of God. I got a glimpse of Him, and it served as an appetizer that made me

81

hungry for more. Every revelation of God makes us hungry for more of Him. The more we taste of Him, the more we want! Since He is infinite, we will spend the rest of eternity getting to know Him, and our understanding of His nature will continually grow. We will be constantly amazed with each new revelation throughout eternity. There will always be deeper realms of the Lord to discover.

Each of us has an opinion, and no one intentionally holds an opinion they believe is wrong! This includes opinions of what God would look like if He literally walked into a church. But God is asking us to lay down our opinions so that He can reveal more of Himself to us. Rigidly held opinions always kill fresh moves of the Spirit.

After pondering this for several months, I began to see that not recognizing the Lord when He appeared may point to a pattern in Scripture. **Whenever God appeared in a form that was initially unrecognized, many times a major transition in His Kingdom would follow**. God showed up in an unexpected form "tipping His hand" that He was about to do business in an entirely different way.

Scripture is replete with examples. Moses spotted a bush that was on fire but not consumed. He investigated. The possibility never entered Moses' mind that he was about to discover God in such a way that would not only change him forever, but would also set an entire nation free. He was quickly confronted with a choice: *Okay, I did not initially recognize this as God, but now that I know it is, what do I do?*

God revealed Himself in an unrecognizable form at first. The result was a radical shift in Moses' awareness of who God really is. Interestingly, it also totally altered the course of history.

Joshua scouted the city of Jericho. A man approached dressed in military attire. Not recognizing this man, Joshua aggressively pulled his sword and demands, "Are you for me, or are you against me?" The man replied, "I am the Captain of the Lord's army." It was God – but Joshua did not recognize Him.

Joshua had history with God. He walked with Moses and witnessed the lightning, the thunder, and the glory shining on Moses' face after meeting with God. We can safely assume Joshua knew what God looked like and how He manifested His presence. Still, when God showed up, Joshua had to ask, "Who are you? Are you for me or against me?" Once he recognized God, guess what followed? God entirely changed how He interacted with Israel. Their goals and objectives totally changed, from getting out of Egypt to conquering the Promised Land.

The most dramatic unrecognized revelation of God was in Jesus' life. Jesus came as the Messiah. Those devoted to God, the people who had history with God, the people who knew Scripture, totally missed the very event they were earnestly looking for! As easy as it is to criticize, it would be wise to learn from their mistake. The Pharisees knew Scripture so well, they could open a scroll at random, read a few words, close the scroll and quote the rest of the passage from memory. They knew the prophecies concerning the Messiah, yet they did not recognize Him when He was in their midst. When God became flesh, it was a paradigm-crushing event. They failed to recognize Him and missed the greatest change of all time.

Just before yet another major shift in the Kingdom, Jesus died and was buried. When He came back from the dead, did anyone immediately recognize Him? Jesus appeared to Mary, one of His closest friends. If anyone should recognize Him, it would be Mary – but she did not recognize Him initially.

Then Jesus appeared to the disciples on the shore. While they fished, Jesus called out, *"Cast your net on the other side of the boat."* As they obeyed, they hauled in a load of fish. It was only then that John suddenly recognized Jesus saying, "Peter, it is the Lord."

Another time two disciples were on the road to Emmaus. Jesus began walking along conversing with them. The disciples told this stranger all the news about Jesus' recent death. Funny…they talked to Jesus about Jesus! I wonder how Jesus held back the laughter! It was as if He was a visitor who needed to catch up on the local news. But they were strangely attracted to Him, realizing that the presence and words of this newcomer warmed their hearts. They broke bread together. Shocked, they realized, *That was the Lord!* And then He disappeared.

Jesus, after the Resurrection, appeared unrecognized to many. What immediately followed? God changed everything He was doing on the planet.

Here is a final example. The Holy Spirit burst in upon 120 people praying in an upper room with the mighty rushing wind, the apparent drunkenness, the appearance of fire on top of their heads. And what did Jerusalem do? They rushed toward the commotion shouting, *"What is this? What is going on?"* God moved and they initially failed to recognize it as the Lord, and yet history changed so dramatically that we are still living out the implications of that day.

There seems to be a pattern. God came to me and I didn't recognize Him initially. Could it be that He is telegraphing a new move? Could it be He is hinting that He is about to shift the way He is going to move in the Earth in the near future?

The first question many would ask me was *"What does Jesus look like?"* Pretty good question! The problem is, the more I tried to describe Him, the more I found myself at a total loss for words. This quickly became quite frustrating. After several unsuccessful attempts to articulate what happened to me, I finally gained some understanding.

He spoke, *"If I were to give you the ability to describe Me perfectly, many people would be satisfied in your explanation and would not press in to their own encounter. I didn't allow you to experience Me merely to explain it to others, but to invite others into their own experience."*

1 John 3:2 says, "We know when He is revealed, we will be like Him for we shall see Him as He is." The goal of Christianity is to become like Jesus. Like you, I have tried this with varying degrees of success. Nothing accelerates the process of conforming to His image more than actually seeing Him. God

85

invites you to come and encounter deeper revelations of His character!

You will never become what I behold. You will only become what you behold. 1 Corinthians 3:18 says, "We all with unveiled faces, beholding as in a mirror the glory of God are being transformed into the same image from glory to glory ... "

God invites us to know Him and move into greater revelation of not only Himself, but of His plans and purposes for our lives. **All of His activity comes out of His divine nature**. It is from partaking of His divine nature[1] that our lives gain meaning and purpose. Daniel prophesied that the people who know God would "be strong and carry out great exploits."[2] In other words, out of intimacy we accomplish great things for God. Like the apostle Paul, my cry is to "know Him and the power of His resurrection and the fellowship of His suffering."[3]

He is calling each individual, and His Body as a whole, into such greatness. What God has destined for us is beyond our wildest imagination. But first, we must see Him. We must seek His face. Perhaps He is inviting you, right now, to see Him as He really is. Are you ready? Do you want to see the King?

---

[1] 2 Peter 1:4
[2] Daniel 11:32
[3] Philippians 3:10

Chapter 6
The Lion's Roar

Then one of the elders said to me, "Do not weep! See, the Lion of the tribe of Judah, the Root of David, has triumphed."
Revelation 5:5

Suddenly, before my eyes, Jesus began to transform into a lion. It was the most majestic, regal and magnificent lion I have ever seen. He was sitting composed and confident, looking over His creation. His eyes seemed to see everything. His chest was very broad and His mane was flowing in the wind. As I watched, the lion opened its mouth to roar, but I heard no sound. Though I saw it rather than heard it, this roar shook me for hours afterwards. It felt as if the molecules in my body were being rearranged.

As I stood before the Lord, He changed before my eyes. He transformed from human form into the most imperial, the most majestic, the most vibrant creature I have ever seen or imagined: the Lion of Judah.

I vividly remember His magnificent head turning as He surveyed all of His creation in a sweeping gaze. His tremendous mane was flowing in the gentle wind. The substance of His royal character was overwhelming. In an instant, I could easily see that He was indeed the King of Kings. His eyes were piercing and all seeing. His ears heard everything. Not one thing in all of creation escaped Him. He ruled with a calm and stately supremacy. His broad, golden chest made me realize that one pounce, one roar, and His enemies would be powerless and have no option but to submit immediately. Nothing could withstand this Mighty King as He looked over all of His creation. He was indeed the Ruler of all; the picture of total dominion. But He did not pounce, because He was preparing to do something else. He moved into position, opened His massive jaw, tilted His royal head and began to roar.

As I watched Him roar, I was overwhelmed with the reverberation of that noise. Keep in mind, I only *saw* Him roar. While I did not hear the actual sound of His roar, it had definite effects throughout my entire body, soul and spirit. Perhaps it was God's kindness that kept me from hearing the sound, or maybe I only needed to see the roar to get the full effect.

Nevertheless, I felt as if my very DNA was being reorganized in that moment. Kathi Oates, who stayed by my side during the entire encounter, later told me that at one point, I began to shake and tremble unnaturally. For the rest of that day and well into the next, I shook uncontrollably. Occasionally, even to this day, I still tremble as I feel something like an electrical current surging through my nerve endings.

In Genesis, Jacob blessed Judah: "You are a lion's cub, O Judah; you return from the prey, my son. Like a lion he crouches and lies down, like a lioness – who dares to rouse him?"[1] The nation of Israel and the people of God are often symbolized by a lion for its sovereignty, strength and courage. In Revelation, Jesus is referred to as the Lion of Judah.[2]

---

[1] Genesis 49:9
[2] Revelation 5:5

The implications of applying this dramatic metaphor to both God **and** His people are sobering and exhilarating. We are His lioness, His Bride, taking after the true Lion King, learning to subdue the enemy, enforcing His authority on Earth and feasting on an inheritance that is already ours. We "re-present" the dominion of His kingdom. People of royal descent behave differently than "commoners." We do not move in our royalty with arrogance but with confidence and assurance. As the Bride of the King we are royalty, and must boldly conduct ourselves accordingly.

Humanity was created and placed in the Garden to please God. God's pleasure was that we would live in intimacy with Him and exercise dominion over the entire planet. The Lord's original intent was for us to steward the earth for Him, thus, by divine design, we were created to have dominion. Just as the lion is considered the "king of the jungle," our mandate as those who rule on His behalf, is to carry out His desires and designs. Dominion is a major principle of kingdom life. If multiple kingdoms exist, the question arises: which king will ultimately hold sway? If we believe in opposing kingdoms, then we must believe there is an enormous fight for control. Which kingdom will prevail in a region is not just a **part** of the issue. It is **the** issue.

Recently I watched an interesting documentary that brought even more understanding. On this particular show, lions were hunting in the grasslands of Africa. The narrator made a statement that was very revealing about the Lord.

He explained that male lions rarely hunt for themselves. Rather, they partner with their pride. When it comes time to hunt, the male lion's contribution to the partnership is simply to roar. Those who have heard a lion roar will testify that there is no other sound like it. It strikes terror so great that their prey becomes senseless with panic and let down their defenses. In a state of terrified shock, the prey does not exercise normal levels of caution. It is at that point that the lionesses do their part. The pride goes in for the kill. The male lion's roar is simply the terrifying distraction allowing the lionesses to partner with him and exercise dominion. It is a genuine partnership.

Jesus, the King, is looking for those who will partner with Him. When the King of Kings roars, He strikes fear in all His enemies – not flesh and blood, but principalities, powers, and rulers of the darkness of this age.[1] **The good news of the King's domain is that the victory has already been won**. It has been said that we do not fight **for** victory, but **from** victory. The King has roared. It is time for the church, His lioness, to partner with Him and enforce His dominion on the planet. We were created by God to exercise His dominion over all things on the earth. The earth belongs to the Lord, and it is time to take back from the enemy what rightfully belongs to the Creator. This is why Paul says in Romans that all of creation eagerly waits for the sons of God to be revealed.[2] Creation belongs to God. He died to purchase it back from the dominion of the Evil One. It is time to go in for the kill and bring a cultural impact that ushers in His dominion in all the earth.

The church often aims too low because we do not think like lionesses but more like common house cats. We have

---

[1] Ephesians 6:12
[2] Romans 8:19

reduced our expectation to a desperate hope that people "pray the prayer," join the church, and then maybe attend regularly and give money. We might even hope to send a few radically committed people out as missionaries to various nations. We feed the poor and help the needy. We start ministries, prayer meetings, and "felt-need" programs. In America, "church success" is often measured by the buildings we build, budgets we maintain and how many people we can gather into our mega-churches.

These things are very good in their proper place, but they are just not enough. **Settling for the "good" when we have greatness within is simply stopping short of what is rightfully ours.** God is not interested in just a few victories, even though He celebrates each one with us. He is interested in building a people who will go in for the kill after His enemies are stricken with terror.

Israel is the Old Testament picture of this principle. They were not led to the Promised Land just to take a few cities, set up a blissful coexistence with the pagan citizens of Canaan, and adopt a toleration of their culture and their gods. Rather, they were commanded to conquer the entire land and utterly annihilate Canaanite culture.[1] They were to dominate and occupy their new territory. God had Israel establish a radically different culture from what previously existed in Canaan. The entire story line of the Old Testament is a fight for the dominion of a kingdom and a culture that originated in the heart of God. It would have been short-sighted for Israel to settle for winning a few battles when God's goal was to establish a kingdom. This is the reality in which we find ourselves this very day.

---

[1] Deuteronomy 7

It is no longer enough to grow big churches and produce nice people. We are betrothed to a Lion! We were sent out to take over the culture. This is the heart of apostolic people. We are the "sent ones" who are to go ahead of the King preparing the way for His return. Our goal is nothing short of maximum socio-cultural impact. Our mandate is to bring heaven's culture to our world, so much so that, when the King sets foot on the planet, He says "Wow, this feels a lot like home!" This is why we were instructed by Jesus to pray, "Thy Kingdom come, Thy will be done, on earth as it is in heaven."[1] If we pray for it, let us also aim for it. Let us not aim too low!

Beloved, we have an opportunity to experience glory before eternal glory! God is extending to us the invitation to experience heaven before heaven. The reality that we have been made to sit together in the heavenly places in Christ Jesus[2] must constantly grow larger until it becomes the exclusive paradigm through which we see life. **We do not have to tolerate a mere earthly existence. We genuinely are spiritual beings, presently sitting together with Christ Jesus in heavenly places**! This truth, once appropriated, changes everything.

We live in an unprecedented hour of church history. There are documented reports of signs and wonders happening all around the world. People are being healed en masse, having stunning prophetic experiences and witnessing

---

[1] Matthew 6:9
[2] Ephesians 2:6

signs in nature. Credible sources report numbers of people being raised from the dead. As recently as a few years ago, many were asking why greater numbers of people were healed in other nations compared to the U.S. This is no longer the case. People are currently being healed in the U.S. with greater regularity.

For some, there is a legitimate concern over charlatan "faith healers" and false prophets. The concern over the counterfeit has created a mindset that throws out the truth in order to keep from being deceived. The counterfeit of those who bring glory to themselves through false miracles and false prophecy is proof which points to the fact that genuine miracles and prophecy exist. Unlike false prophets and apostles, genuine displays of supernatural power result in Jesus being glorified and praised. This is precisely what the Holy Spirit is doing in this season, and many are being converted!

Earth is beginning to look like heaven as God's people refuse to settle for inferior experiences with Him. We have a long way to go, but we have come a long way. Church alone no longer satisfies and there is a remnant of God's people and local churches who are partnering with God for more! In response, He is releasing unprecedented signs and wonders – and it will only increase. What a wonderful day to be alive, a day in which we can fully enter into what Daniel, Ezekiel, Jeremiah and Isaiah glimpsed, but longed to see more clearly.

Segments of the Body of Christ are already moving into higher levels of victory and dominion. Advancements are coming more quickly than ever. These experiences are not being made available to simply thrill a few bored Christians. The Lord is much too strategic for that, and the time is far too

93

short. Deeper revelation and experience of God's power are not limited to a special class of Christian. Anyone who comes with the innocence of a child can access deeper revelation from the Lord. These types of encounters are not God's stamp of approval on an individual or a ministry. We already possess every spiritual blessing in heavenly places.[1] If it is a blessing, and it is from heaven, it is ours! We are now simply accessing what has already been delivered to us.

It is expected that people in every sphere of society will infiltrate their sector with kingdom realities. For years, if a person came to the pinnacle of spiritual maturity, it was assumed that they would leave their "secular" employment and surrender to vocational ministry. That day is over! **Live it out wherever God has positioned you.** Everyone has a mandate to influence their sector of society: business owners, politicians, millionaires, medical professionals, educators, entertainers. We are commissioned for international impact…outside the walls of "church!"

This is not too big a task for us, because we are a people of power. The apostle Paul tells us that we can do all things through Christ who strengthens us.[2] This truth also issues quite a challenge. It means that I am a person of power – a person who "can do all things." If I **can** do all things and I am **not** doing all things, then something has gone awry. It means I need a new mindset. If we truly can do all things through Christ, we can no longer blame people, circumstances, or lack of resources. We have that much dominion within us!

---

[1] Ephesians 1:3
[2] Philippians 4:13

◆◆◆

God is increasing our ability to see what He sees. These astonishing supernatural experiences are so rich; they release fresh revelation of the Lord Jesus Christ and insight into His plans and purposes for us individually and corporately. This is producing great love and passion for the Lord Jesus.

It is time to be a royal person of dominion. In every place we walk, we bring the Lord calm and stately majesty. We have all of heaven's resources. Now, we need to fill our hearts with confidence and boldly ask, *God, open the heavens! Let me see the King in His glory. Let me take my place of authority! The Lion of Judah roar, and I will partner with Him!*

Chapter 7
Releasing the Spirit's Fire

Dear friends, if our hearts do not condemn us, we have
confidence before God and receive from him anything we ask,
because we obey his commands and do what pleases him. And
this is his command: to believe in the name of his Son, Jesus
Christ, and to love one another ...
1 John 3:21

Then he asked me if I wanted to see what the Lord
was doing in Anápolis. I said yes. He gave me a wide-angle,
aerial view of the city of Anápolis. Suspended above it was a
giant ball of fire. It was the fire of revival and a giant move
of His Spirit ready to be released, yet still hanging above the
city in a giant net. The giant orb strained to break through
the net, but was constrained by the crisscrossed ropes. Every
once in a while a fragment of the fireball would drop through
the net and touch people. At times bigger pieces of fire
would fall – but the enormous bulging mass of fire was still
hanging suspended, prevented from falling by the net that
restrained it.

Then the angel asked me if I wanted to see the net
that was stopping the ball of fire from falling. I said yes. He
brought me close enough to see the net. The crisscrossed
cables that composed the net had two different phrases
written on them – UNFORGIVENESS AND BROKEN
RELATIONSHIPS. In other words, if unforgiveness and
broken relationships were not there, there would be no net
restraining the Spirit's fire from falling in Anápolis.

For some time after returning from my trip, I thought this last segment of the experience stood alone. Thank God, He helped me avoid what could have been a tragic mistake! At first, I erroneously believed this was a message exclusively for the city of Anápolis, Brazil. *Later, I realized that this was actually the lynchpin connecting the entire encounter.* This revelation is what releases the fire, not just to an individual, but to entire regions. It also contains the greatest challenge.

In the first part of this experience, fire prepared me to see Jesus face to face. In the second part, fire prepares an entire region to see the Lord. Here is what the Lord later revealed: **What God allowed me to experience on an individual level, entire regions can experience on massive levels.** This, then, became a strategic key to unlock deeper experiences in God over entire regions.

In Brazil, the same day this all happened, Randy asked me to share this part of the experience at the evening crusade meeting. Shaking and barely coherent, I stood before more than 5,000 and related, as best I could, what I had seen over their city. As I stood to speak, angels lined the back of the large auditorium, each with a pair of scissors in hand. They were eager to cut the ropes of unforgiveness and bitterness that had restrained the fire of God over their city.

After sharing, I asked people to repent of unforgiveness and broken relationships. It was quite clear that widespread, regional breakthrough would ensue. But, at the conclusion of the invitation, only a handful responded. I attempted to hand the microphone back to Randy, who handed it back to me saying,

"Try again!" I repeated the invitation, but only a few more responded. I was weak and shaky, and my physical strength was giving way, so I handed the microphone back to Randy. He explained the importance of this invitation to the crowd, but still the response was limited.

As I considered the limited response, God gave me understanding. He said, **"If I had asked my church to do something difficult, they would have done it."** The Lord showed me that if a move of the Spirit was guaranteed after a prolonged fast, they would eagerly fast. If a Pentecost experience was guaranteed after praying around the clock for 40 days, they would gladly pray. People volunteer freely for what they view as a heroic, ultimate or extreme spiritual act. But, the response was minimal because **most people believe the realm of relationships is not that spiritual.**

The Old Testament account of Naaman, commander of the Syrian army, illustrates that *people would rather perform extreme acts of spiritual heroism than acts of simple obedience*.[1] Namaan had leprosy. A Jewish servant girl suggested that he contact the prophet in Israel. Naaman hooked up the horses, gathered his entourage and, amid much fanfare, went to Elisha's house. Elisha didn't even bother to answer the door! Instead, he sent word to Naaman instructing him to dip seven times in the Jordan River. Indignation overtook Naaman because of Elisha's unceremonious treatment and mundane instructions. Offended, Naaman turned to leave. The instructions Elisha gave Naaman felt very unspiritual to him. They seemed beneath him.

---

[1] 2 Kings 5

His men implored, "My father, if the prophet had told you to do something great, would you not have done it?" Naaman eventually yielded to his men, obeyed the simple command, and was totally healed.

Undervaluing relationships as mundane and unspiritual was precisely why I thought this last part of the encounter was completely separate, and also why the response at the crusade was so limited. A great heroic quest amid fanfare, or a super-spiritual feat demonstrating heroic commitment and extreme zeal would have at least **felt** spiritual. Relationships, however, can feel very unspiritual. They are tangible – you live with them day to day. Relationships are not a one-time, heroic task, but a daily humbling process of learning to love.

What if there had been a collective, immediate, zealous repentance in Brazil that night? Would the angels have cut the cords of the net and let the fire fall? Would God have opened the eyes of all who gathered there? Would God have overwhelmingly met those needing healing and deliverance? Would the bitterness of broken relationships have melted under the power of His love and tenderness? Taking it one step further, would God have moved so powerfully among the unchurched throughout the city that they would be unexplainably impacted where they sat – in restaurants, bars, living rooms, cars or buses?

There is a powerful regional release of the Spirit as God's children get along. This release not only impacts the church, but entire populations. The Bible supports the idea that unity in the church can result in powerful regional outpourings of His Spirit. Unity is so high-impact that, what happens in a specific meeting can effect unsuspecting people who are not even seeking God.

This entire dynamic is played out in the birth of the Church. At Passover, Jesus told 500 to go wait in Jerusalem until Pentecost.[1] By the time Pentecost came, there were only 120 left in that upper room. What happened to the other 380? What occurred in that upper room[2] over those several weeks?

Use your imagination for a moment. You have spent three years of your life following Jesus. You have learned to trust Him as He taught and demonstrated truths about His kingdom. The group you traveled with, however, was fairly dysfunctional. They were always arguing about who was greatest and who would get to sit next to Jesus in His kingdom.

Jesus told your small group to go wait in Jerusalem for the "Holy Spirit," which was totally foreign to you. He was then brutally and unexpectedly executed. Depression, bewilderment, despair and fear abounded. But as instructed, you went to Jerusalem with 499 other people in the same disappointing plight. Everyone was dealing with grief, sudden loss of leadership and fear of the occupying government, not to mention the inadequate facilities!

But, as instructed, you wait… and wait…. All these discomforts were compounded by the fact that now you were in a prayer meeting without the Holy Spirit. We can think of few things more excruciating than being in a prayer meeting without the Holy Spirit! Yet, here were 500 disillusioned, beleaguered, expressive Mediterraneans – all in one stuffy, hot, overcrowded room praying – without the Holy Spirit. Yuck!

---

[1] Acts 1:4-7
[2] Acts 1:13

100

What happened in the weeks between the resurrection and Pentecost? I wonder if any of the 500 gave up prematurely. Perhaps some started shaking a little, leapt to their feet and said, "Well, I have the Holy Spirit now. Catch you guys later." Or, "Hey – did you feel that? I got a goose bump!" (rolling up the sleeve of his robe for a closer examination). Whatever the case, eventually 380 succumbed to one thing or another.

Regardless, as this process of attrition played out, one thing definitely transpired: **they worked out their relationships**. In low times, offense and hurt feelings abound. This was sure to have been the case in the upper room. Perhaps James came to Peter humbly, saying something like, "Peter, I have been offended with you for being such a loudmouth. It's my sin and I take full responsibility for it. Will you forgive me?" Perhaps Martha humbled herself before her little sister, "Mary, please forgive me for harboring bad feelings about you. All those times you were at the Lord's feet…I thought you were just kissing up. I take full responsibility for my negative feelings. I'm sorry."

What happened to all the squabbling about who was greatest? During those days of waiting they gained an understanding of each other and came to a rock solid, covenant type of commitment: "We are not leaving this room until God does something in all of us. We stand or fall together."

Finally, after a process of almost two months, God had His desire: 120 out of the original 500 were ruggedly committed to each other. They were all "with one accord in one place."[1] It was **at that point** that the Holy Spirit rushed in with a mighty wind and tongues of fire. The move of the Spirit was so powerful that people who were not in the meeting came running to that

---

[1] Acts 2:1

sound! The 120 coming into unity released such a move of God that it impacted the entire region.

Could it be that during those tense weeks in the upper room, angels with scissors were cutting away the cords of unforgiveness and broken relationships? Could it be the last 'snip' intentionally coincided with "when the day of Pentecost was fully come?" The final broken relationship was healed, the final rope of bitterness was cut, and the Holy Spirit rushed in with vehement power. As a result, the entire region was impacted and human history was changed forever.

God cannot and will not stay away from a place of worship and covenant friendship. Christians today want the Acts 2 experience of Pentecost without the discomfort and responsibility of getting into one accord. It is easy to be in one accord theoretically with the universal church … just not with a local church you have to see daily! What would happen if God asked you to take a couple months off work and sit in a room with the people you go to church with until the Holy Spirit comes in power? Spectator Christianity would come to the quick and violent end it deserves!

God is looking for people who will diligently love each other. Through the energetic embracing of differences and a diligence to keep short accounts with each other, this much needed mindset will be forged: **"We live together, and we die together."** Our unity will be based upon God's type of love and covenant commitments.

The process of getting into one accord is difficult but not impossible. Conflicts among Christians do not need to be lethal or permanent. They are wonderful opportunities for relationships to deepen and for new levels of honor and respect to develop. Relationships do not increase in depth or meaning until they have worked through conflict. Those who shun conflict, or do not know how to embrace it and work through it, often end up confused, choosing to wander away from their God-given spiritual families.

This tendency to wander rather than persevere in covenant relationships has produced a society where life-long commitments are rare. Undervaluing such commitments has infused the church with the consumer culture of the world, producing Christians who church hop, nonchalantly tossing aside the relationships of a spiritual family. Learning to stand alongside one another through differences and difficulties creates a depth of intimacy, mutual respect and honor that is priceless and powerful. Resolved issues leave the heart open to greater depths of relational intimacy.

Restoring relationships is not easy. We have a real enemy who is desperate with fear over the idea of Christians walking in love and harmony. We cannot afford to take the easy route. There is too much at stake and the benefits are too precious. By our unity, we can be a genuine blessing to this planet. We will become a source of inheritance for others in our regions. Others will benefit from our covenant affection and begin to have supernatural experiences without having had to gain this ground for themselves. Through unity, the Holy Spirit is free to reveal a deeper understanding of Jesus both to you, and to your region.

◆◆◆

103

A few years ago, I heard my friend and author of *Experiencing Father's Embrace*, the late Jack Frost, heralding that we are in the midst of a revival of the love of God. This "Agape Reformation" is a grand, sweeping movement of the love of God that will be as profound and far-reaching as the Protestant Reformation.

I believe there are two facets to this Reformation. In the first wave, God will stabilize the heart of the Church in His love. There is nothing greater than experiencing God's affection and being rooted in His love. To fully realize the depths of God's love results in confidence, deep devotion and passion for Jesus. In the second wave, our love for one another will be fully manifest. Jesus said this is how those who followed Him would be known. Supernatural love for each other will emerge from the healed hearts of people in the Body of Christ who are committed to one another in ironclad affection. The Lord is offering both supernatural and relational prosperity in this second facet of the Agape Reformation. This double-portion prosperity is not from the world. It is the prosperity of the kingdom. We attain this prosperity the same way that Job attained his: by praying for his friends![1]

Through this encounter the Lord ultimately revealed to me that if we take the first step toward resolving issues of unforgiveness and broken relationships, it will result in powerful moves of God affecting entire regions. The potential for greater and deeper experiences in His supernatural kingdom will be realized. While this is simple, it is simply powerful. There is a great open door of opportunity to reconcile all uncomfortable

---

[1] Job 42:10

104

relationships, drop every quarrel,[1] and, to the extent possible, live at peace with everyone.[2] We have the confidence to receive anything we ask because we keep His commandments and do those things that are pleasing in His sight.[3] "This is His commandment: that we should believe on the name of His Son, Jesus Christ, and love one another ..."[4]

Let no relationship be exempt. As much as it depends on you, be at peace with all men. Realistically, there are those with whom no further relationship is possible at this point. These you can forgive, quickly, easily and graciously, with a phone call or visit. For others, forgiveness will open up an opportunity to draw closer. Either way, will you take the first step toward forgiveness and restoration? Will you take responsibility for broken relationships and let the angels cut away the cords that hold back the fire of God over your region?

---

[1] Colossians 3:13
[2] Romans 12:18
[3] 1 John 3:22
[4] 1 John 3:23

Chapter 8
Let the Heavens Open

The man without the Spirit does not accept the things that come from the Spirit of God, for they are foolishness to him, and he cannot understand them, because they are spiritually discerned.
1 Corinthians 2:14

Within a few months of returning from Brazil, I was outside doing yard work when our home phone rang. My wife answered it and began talking to one of our close friends. She rushed into the front yard with the phone, talking excitedly and looking up at the sky. While looking up, she became very animated. Knowing how calm she tends to be, this piqued my interest. As I looked up, I was absolutely stunned by what I saw over the skies of Sugar Land, Texas! **Around the sun in a perfect circle was the same type of rainbow I had seen on the way to Anápolis!** God once again had my attention! Scientists call this a "halo" rainbow. While they may happen occasionally in other parts of the world – I had never seen one before Brazil. Now I was seeing one over my home town!

My Christian history is filled with lots of reading – about **other** people's miracles, healings, angelic visitations and other supernatural phenomena. To add insult to injury, these accounts were not only about other **people**, they were always about other **places** and other **periods** of time.

Thankfully, I can say that day is over! By giving me this sign in the heavens in my own home town, in my own front yard, I believed that God was making an enticing statement about the possibilities right where I live! He promised to open the heavens once again. Because of what happened to me in Brazil, I was more convinced that God would let me have these types of experiences on mission trips, but remained skeptical that it could happen in my own home town! Now He was bringing it to my front yard! We not only have the privilege of reading other people's history with God in lands far away, we can press in for our own encounters right here at home.

Within the next month, my wife and I piled into our conversion van with our four energetic children and drove to church – our normal, crazy Sunday morning routine. Along the way, I pondered what I was about to share. How much could I tell about the encounter in Brazil? Could I explain that, during the encounter, I did not know whether I was in my body or out of my body?[1] Would they think I had lost my mind? Would transformation show in my appearance or demeanor? Would anyone sense that I had changed as much as I felt I had? It is, after all, impossible to stay the same after an experience of this nature. I didn't **want** to stay the same! Was it too much to hope that my friends would step into a covenant agreement with me, and that we could walk into the depths of the supernatural realm together?

As I shared the story at our church that Sunday morning, something significant began among us that day, and continues to this day. Sharing my experience touched off a transformation in

---

[1] 2 Corinthians 12:3

our congregation, just as I was transformed in Brazil. **The telling of my story opened the door for others to have similar experiences in my church!** Not only is this happening in my local church, but as I travel through the United States and other nations, it happens there as well.

We must understand that there is great power in the words of our testimony. Testimonies change spiritual realities by granting our hearts a taste of what is possible in any given moment. The power of testimony is demonstrated when faith ignites our hearts as we listen to others share their stories. The stories of God's activity were vital to the Israelites in the Old Testament and to the early church as well. Our testimony actually changes the spiritual atmosphere and causes realities to shift. Testimonies grant access to others so that they, too, may experience what we just described.

Revelation 19:10 records that "the testimony of Jesus is the spirit of prophecy." When we report what the Lord has done, it creates a prophetic environment in which faith grows, such that our experience can be repeated in the lives of others.

There is a difference between **history** and **testimony**. History describes where we have been; testimony describes what God is doing. Many Christians are living on their history in God – what He did months, or even years ago. History is important, but God wants us to have a current testimony of His activity in our lives.

I so wanted my friends at church to experience what I had received in Brazil. The words of Paul in his letter to the

Romans reverberated in my mind, "*I long to see you so that I may impart to you some spiritual gift to make you strong – that is, that you and I may be mutually encouraged by each other's faith.*"[1] I had received a powerful impartation, and since I had received it so freely, I wanted to give it away freely.

At the close of the service, I invited those who wanted to stay for a prayer of impartation to come forward. **Nearly everyone in the congregation came up for prayer.** As we prayed through lunch and late into the afternoon, I asked God to open our eyes and draw us into a fresh revelation of the King and His kingdom. I prayed that my friends' eyes would be open to see the multitude of angels surrounding us.[2] God moved powerfully that day and granted my heart's desire that we would all begin this journey together.

After that impartation service, I began to hear stories from people that God was doing in others what He had done in me! Below are just some of the stories that came immediately to me.

At one of our services, one woman, a hair designer and mother of one small child, fell and wept under the ministry of the Holy Spirit. At one point she actually saw the feet of Jesus right beside her. She said they were so real that she reached out to touch them and thought she would literally be able to feel them. Lying on the floor for quite some time, she wept and called the Lord's name. She repeatedly stretched out her hand attempting to touch the Lord's feet. She came to church that day and saw Jesus, rather than just hearing words spoken about Him. She was

---

[1] Romans 1:11
[2] 2 Kings 6:16-17

among the first of many whose eyes and ears were opened to the spiritual realm of the King's domain.

A three-year-old member of our congregation was with his mom in the preschool area of church one evening. At one point during the service, he said to his mother, "Mommy, let's go look at the angels!" He led his mom by the hand into the auditorium and began pointing, "There's one! There's one!"

His mother recognized a teachable moment that could either turn her son towards the spiritual realities or away from them. She wisely responded, "Mommy doesn't see them, but that doesn't mean they're not there. Show me all the angels." The boy pointed out the "blue-green angels" all over the auditorium. Next, he pulled his mother out into the parking lot and began to point them out there, too. I have heard that blue-green, or turquoise, represents intercession. Interestingly, that evening there was extra grace on us in the area of prayer. Needless to say, three-year-olds are not yet psychologically predisposed to make up something like this!

Another child, an eight-year-old in our church, came up to me one day and told me that when I was on the platform she saw "sparkles" all around me. "Sparkly angels" is a term I have heard some young children use.

Angels sometimes appeared in our services and literally left white feathers behind. Not all angels have feathers, but some do. On many occasions, when I have been preaching or leading worship, white feathers will fall in front of me. After teaching a class on prophetic worship, our trumpet player found a large white feather on his trumpet case. There are many reports of people seeing feathers in their homes. It happens quite frequently. At strategic moments, feathers fall from "nowhere." While this will be a stretch for many in westernized churches, whenever we see them, it brings our attention to heaven and we glorify Jesus!

During one worship service, the auditorium lights were dimmed, with only the stage lights on. Suddenly, angels began to fill the room and the auditorium started radiating gold. When that happened, an overwhelming sense of awe filled the place. On other occasions, gold dust has appeared on people's hands from out of no where. Many in the congregation have witnessed gold dust falling from their clothing when they stood up.

One night in particular stands out in which several people heard the same supernatural sound at the exact same time. A woman in our congregation was standing in front of the sound booth during a Friday evening worship service. Suddenly, she began to hear a choir singing, in tight harmony with perfect pitch. She kept looking behind her for the source of the unbelievably beautiful music. She knew that what she was hearing could not be originating from the stage! God was granting her access to hear into the angelic realm despite the racket the rest of us were making.

Being a very quiet, analytical type of person, such an experience was quite out of character. Nonetheless, she mustered the courage and testified about that experience during our very next Sunday morning service. Later the same day, I received the

111

following e-mail from another who had also heard the exact same singing!

> "When I came to the service that Friday night, I was sitting right behind the lady who shared. At one point in worship, when I had my head down and my eyes closed, I felt as though heaven had come down. The power and presence of God were so strong. Suddenly, the voices became heavenly. I remember thinking that these were the most beautiful voices I had ever heard. Their harmony and tone were heavenly. I remember thinking and asking the Lord if these were angels. I pondered this experience later, and was almost willing to dismiss it because I thought it was my imagination and that I was being too spiritual. But because it was shared from the platform later on, it confirmed to me that angels had indeed come to join in our worship. I remembered what you shared about how we are taught to dismiss supernatural things as just imagination and I realized that I was indeed hearing into the angelic realm. God is so good. Wow! I heard angels!"

But this story continues. While these two women were hearing the same angelic sounds, yet another member of our church, the wife of the leader of our prophetic ministries, was running the sound board that evening. **She started hearing the same angelic choir**. The voices were so distinct that she tried turning knobs and pushing buttons to adjust the sound in the house speakers and in the monitors. She kept making adjustments wondering where these new sounds were coming from! Finally, she realized that the sounds did not originate from our stage but from heaven!

After that initial impartation service, a single woman had an angelic encounter. One particularly difficult day she went to bed discouraged. She was awakened in the middle of the night by a man surrounded by bright light standing in her room. Now that gets one's attention, especially if you're a single woman. The man said, "Hey, do you remember that part in Acts when there was a storm at sea and an angel stood by Paul and strengthened him?" She answered, "Yeah." The man replied, "Well, this is that!" And then he disappeared!

Secure in the fact that God knew her name and address and dispatched an angel to strengthen her, she fell into a peaceful sleep. She woke up refreshed and strengthened, the discouragement broken.

Our church has by no means arrived. We are still on the journey. The glory ebbs and flows. Rather than focusing on what is lacking during the "low tide," we celebrate what is happening and testify of what the Holy Spirit is doing. What God is doing is tremendous and we will feed ourselves on His faithfulness! We are at the beginning of the beginning, with so much more to experience together.

I offer the testimony of our church as a launching pad from which you can take off into even greater realms. As you do, others may have the opportunity to come alongside you and inherit what you are gaining in your journey. The principle of sonship and inheritance is simply this: we receive rewards we

113

did not work for, simply based upon our relationship as a son or daughter. You will receive my rewards as you place your heart under the ministry of this testimony. Others will receive your rewards as they relate to you and your testimony.

Since that day in Anápolis when I encountered the angel, I have had several opportunities to share my testimony outside our church. The response to this story has amazed me. People are being transformed as they encounter God for themselves. It is wonderful! We are living what used to be just a dream.

Deeper experiences with God are available for anyone who wants to enter in. They are the inheritance of every believer. They are normal Christianity. What was normal for the believers to experience in the book of Acts is available to us today – and more.

I am confident that many of you are going to begin experiencing heavenly realities today, simply because you are reading the words of these testimonies, which is the spirit of prophecy. Many of you will be launched into a season of acceleration. Nothing will remain the same.

Our story is just that: **our story**. The question that now remains for you is this: what will **your** story be? The greatest stories are yet to be written. The greatest wealth of the church still lies dormant within the hearts of many believers who sit in their congregations, week in and week out. There are no God-imposed limitations. The plans He has for you are bigger than you have dared to dream. What testimonies await as you say "yes" to the invitation of the Spirit to walk into greater supernatural realities? We are the history-makers who will usher in the restoration of normal spirituality, born for this amazing moment!

Chapter 9
The Journey in the Depths

When He, the Spirit of truth, has come, He will guide you into
all truth.
John 16:13

How does one process a "suddenly of God?"

Can you imagine what Israel felt when Pharaoh's army backed them into a corner at the Red Sea? The options were to either go swimming or have a very unpleasant reunion! Suddenly, the sea parted and they were looking at dry land. For us, the choice looks logical, but for them, walking across the sea floor between two enormous walls of water held up by an unseen force was an act of total trust. They were literally walking upon their encounter with God. Limited options certainly make some choices easier!

Even after God encounters us and opens new doors of access into supernatural realities, we, like the Israelites, enter a process. Lives are never lived in events, but rather in processes. This is why Paul exhorted Timothy to "make strategies of war"[1] according to the prophetic revelation spoken over his life.

These deeper experiences with God provide a platform from which we can plan our lives, reach our destinies on earth and live in the dream God has in His heart for us. Process is the key to experiencing heaven before heaven. Knowing that every encounter with God is an invitation to an accelerated process, we must embrace a response that helps us maximize each experience with God. Stewardship involves designing responses that

---
[1] 2 Timothy 1

maximize what we have been given. How we steward one encounter greatly affects the timing and release of the next.

Often, after receiving a powerful encounter or deep revelation, our lives take "interesting" turns. These turns are generally not for the better, but seem to be for the worse! Many prophets have uttered promises over our lives, and these are sometimes followed by months and even years of the **complete opposite**. When that happens, our first temptation is to conclude that the word was false and start collecting stones with which to stone the prophet! Yet, in this time of apparent contradiction, God can develop His greatest treasure within us. He brings us to the place of trusting Him regardless of circumstances. These phases of contradiction are the best times to partner with God in bringing forth our individual destiny on the earth. Rather than giving up during these unsettling times, we need to press in!

God uses all types of revelation, and the resulting process to transform our ways of thinking. The Bible calls this "repentance." This was the very heart of both John the Baptist's and Jesus' message: Repent – change your ways of thinking – because the Kingdom is "at hand."[1] With the Kingdom here, now, within our reach, the potential exists to change the way we think, even the most deeply embedded thought patterns and beliefs. The importance of the mind in our walk with God has been underestimated. God values our minds so much that the first word of Jesus' first public sermon dealt with the gray matter between our ears. The way we think leads to attitudes, behaviors and habits that are either in harmony with

---

[1] Matthew 4:17

117

the King's domain or congruent with the ways of the world. God is calling His people to develop a Kingdom paradigm and lifestyle, which can only be done based on repentance.

Repentance used to be defined exclusively as *feel sorry for your sins and turn away from them.* While this is a true application, it is incomplete. Repentance in the fullest sense of the word means come to a new transcendent way of thinking. When repentance is with respect to sin, it means turning away from evil because you have changed your mind. But when repentance is with respect to God's Kingdom, it means changing our entire earthly mindset to a Kingdom paradigm. The Lord wants us thinking in a completely different way. Why? Because, the Kingdom is here. Repentance is necessary to even **see** the Kingdom, and seeing the Kingdom will bring about more repentance. Thus, we find ourselves in a never-ending process of conforming to the image of Jesus – a process that requires careful stewardship.

Stewardship is one of the most prominent keys to the release of more. Processing the supernatural, both personally and corporately, requires attention and diligence. We must treasure and steward every gift from the Lord. When you neglect a gift, you do not give it the attention that it deserves. Neglect is as much an example of poor stewardship as outright waste. God is looking for good stewards who will treasure what He gives – those to whom He can give much, and from whom He can require much.

Is there a protocol for what to do with profound encounters and amazing prophecies? How do we partner with God when our lives seem to unravel? Do angelic visitations and third heaven encounters offer any practical help in our families and places of work? Does God give us these experiences just so we can have an impressive story at the next potluck? Can these encounters help us love people more, the distinction of all true followers of Jesus?[1] Once we have experienced God in this way, do we settle in passively, or do we become active? Is there a required or recommended response? Is there a greater purpose? Is there a process to be entered? Is there some rhyme or reason for these deeper experiences in God?

God is the most intentional Being in the universe. He never does anything haphazardly. God intends encounters to result in transformation. Experiences that only result in momentary diversion and fleeting change are incomplete. God's greater purpose for these types of encounters is to develop greater intimacy with His people and to strategically advance His Kingdom.

Our microwave society has conditioned us to believe that if we could have one major encounter with God, we will have arrived – we will be finished growing. This is not the case. **Every event in the Kingdom leads to a process.**

Scriptural examples are too numerous to list, but Joseph's life story is a prominent example of how supernatural revelation can result in a long and contradictory process. As we live out the process, it leads to more events, which lead to more processes. This is how maturity and advancement in the deeper realms of God are realized. Thus, after an encounter, the way we steward the ensuing process will determine how we advance in God. Life in the Spirit is a journey, an adventure, a process. God

---

[1] John 13:35

119

is vitally interested in the process because this is where we spend time together and learn His heart and His ways.

In the adventure of process, we must become keenly aware that "every good and perfect gift comes from above."[1] Wisdom stewards every gift for what it is: a precious treasure. We are instructed not to neglect the gift that is in us.[2]

The connection between these concepts and what happened to me in Brazil suddenly dropped into place: the heavenly encounter was an infinitely valuable and precious gift from God. I understand that the way in which I steward this gift will be vital to my destiny. I cannot afford to indulge in passivity – there is too much at stake. To "wait and see what happens next" would equate to neglecting this valuable gift – and I determined not to let that happen. This, and all my experiences in God, must enact a practical change in every arena of my life: the way I think, the way I speak, the way I love my friends, the way I treat my family. Wisely stewarding this experience will help ensure that I get the full benefit of the process that began in me that day in Brazil.

Just as God created the world with His word, we create worlds with our words. We either create negative, critical worlds or worlds of praise and thanksgiving. Too many times we focus on what we don't have rather than thanking God for what we already possess. Stewardship begins with celebrating what we have been given. Let thanksgiving be constantly on our lips.

---

[1] James 1:17
[2] 1 Timothy 4:14

120

Rejoice in what God is doing rather than lamenting what you feel is missing. People who complain "I just never get those types of experiences" should not be surprised if they just never get those types of experiences! Good stewardship requires that we refuse to speak words that are contrary to our destiny.

For me, one important way to steward the gift of my encounter was to make a concerted effort to engage in the discipline of writing. As part of the stewardship of this gift, I carefully detailed the experience in my journal. If God is willing to speak, we should at least be willing to write it down! Then I did exactly what scripture instructs: I submitted the revelation to others for their judgment.[1] Interestingly, the Bible never allows a person who receives revelation to judge it for themselves. To discern whether or not this was from God, and what it all meant, was not my job, it was the job of those with whom I am in covenant relationship. Scripture is clear – **others must judge the veracity of our revelation**. I developed a group of trusted friends who are open to whatever God might say and invited their input on the encounter, and the ensuing process.

Stewarding experiences adequately, whether in writing or speaking, requires the use of words. In submitting this to my trusted friends, one hurdle I had to overcome was the gross inadequacy of words to convey the glory of this, or any, supernatural experience. Even the most splendid of descriptions pale compared to the matchless glory of heaven. As we move from glory to glory, words will quite often fail to convey even a fraction of the reality that exists in other dimensions.

---

[1] 1 Corinthians 14:29

The first few times I shared my experience, with one exception in Imperitriz, Brazil, it went over like a lead balloon! The words came out of my mouth and felt as though they fell straight to the ground. The crowd was bored – even I was bored! To this day it is virtually impossible to articulate many parts of this experience. But as I persevere in the process, I am growing in the grace of using woefully inadequate language to capture and impact the hearts of people.

Journeying with God into the depths of the supernatural realm requires us to reclaim our revelatory gifts. It occurred to me in the early days when we began moving in the prophetic that most of us had actually touched deep revelation as children.

The more I thought about it, I realized that I had been having prophetic experiences and supernatural revelations throughout my childhood. But, instead of embracing these events, I simply trained myself to disregard them.

What child has not heard something in their room during the night? What youngster has not seen something in their closet? Desiring to comfort their children, but without an appreciation for spiritual encounters, parents inadvertently taught their children that their perceptions were irrational. They turned on the lights to "prove" that nothing was there, or opened the closet door and demonstrated that it was just their imagination.

This is often the beginning of our schooling in western rationalism, which trains us to doubt our experiences, attributing them to the mere antics of a hyperactive imagination. For most of my childhood, and into my theological training, I believed my eyes were playing tricks on me. My "logic," western rationalism's term for doubt and unbelief, bolted shut the doors

122

to supernatural experiences. The futile thinking of rationalism actually trained me to settle for less than the fullness of God "who could do immeasurably more than all we ask or **imagine**, according to His power that is at work within us."[1]

It is time to retrain ourselves in the innocent belief of early childhood. When young Samuel heard a voice calling his name in the temple, Eli did not respond, "You're just hearing things. Look, I will light this oil lamp and prove no one is there. Your imagination is getting the best of you!"[2] Thankfully, Samuel did not have to "undo" bad teaching based on Eli's lack of understanding of the supernatural. This was a great advantage to him on his journey to becoming one of Israel's great prophets.

And after all, God's sheep hear His voice.[3] As a believer, you have had at least one prophetic experience. You heard his voice drawing you to Himself! This means you can prophesy! Retraining ourselves into Samuel's type of innocent faith would serve us well.

Retraining ourselves out of skepticism will make us less likely to dismiss our supernatural impressions. Instead of waving them away, we will use them as a springboard to engage our hearts in a dialogue with God. The next time you see, hear, taste, smell or feel something, don't write it off so quickly. Begin to train your senses by asking God questions.

Questions from His kids are not problematic for Him. He loves inquiring minds, when they come from innocent belief and

[1] Ephesians 3:14-21
[2] 1 Samuel 3:1-10
[3] John 10:3-5

trust. Dialoguing with God was an area of retraining for me, too, since, for most of my Christian experience I was taught that questions were indicators of doubt and skepticism. Yes - Jesus did react quite negatively to questions from the Pharisees. They asked questions alright, just not from an open, teachable heart desiring to learn, but from a heart that had already formed conclusions. Religious blinders kept them from really learning through dialogue. In contrast, God cannot resist questions from a believing heart. In fact, He loves the conversations.

Daniel is a profoundly instructive example of this. He set his heart to understand what God was doing. He fasted, prayed and asked God questions. In response, God sent Gabriel, one of the only three angels named in the Bible, to give Daniel the "skill to understand."[1] And what an answer he gave! As a result of Daniel engaging his heart in dialogue about things he did not understand, we have the most detailed end time prophecy recorded in scripture! God overwhelmingly demonstrated His generosity with Daniel's request for help understanding His mysteries!

The Kingdom of God is full of mystery, but our Heavenly Father loves to answer us when we ask to understand them. We get the best of both worlds! On one hand, we trust in a God who we cannot fully understand, because He is wonderfully mysterious. On the other hand, we have the privilege of asking Him questions and receiving more understanding of Him. It doesn't get any better than this!

Like Daniel, I had little idea of the full meaning of my experience in Brazil. Over a period of time, in dialogue with God

---

[1] Daniel 9:22

124

and others, more understanding gradually dawned. God is always the best interpreter of God!

This Holy Spirit, who loves to reveal mysteries to the humble heart, lives inside us! No one received a "mini-Holy Spirit!" He is the Spirit of Revelation who was sent to guide us into all truth.[1] He searches the heart of God and discloses to us the deep mysteries that are waiting to be brought to our mind from the fathomless depths of our spirit.[2] Even now, He is waiting for questions from those whose hearts desire to understand.

There was another profoundly practical element in the ensuing process. One of my trusted friends commented, "*What difference does it make if you can see angels and go to the third heaven if it doesn't help you give and receive love among your family and friends in practical ways?*" His question to me was the embodiment of 1 Corinthians 13. Practical love makes the Lord wonderfully pragmatic in all He does – even in heavenly visitations.

When I returned home, I had to wrestle through the practical aspects of my encounter. A personal goal of mine is to live in such a way that the people who are closest to me respect me the most. It is great to preach and gain people's respect from afar, but real fulfillment is when those who know me best have the highest opinion of me. In view of this, it was a great joy and relief to hear those closest to me state that they thought I was radically more loving, peaceful and joyful since I returned from Brazil.

---

[1] John 16:13
[2] 1 Corinthians 2:10

When people fail to embrace the pragmatic side of the supernatural, it is sometimes referred to as being "so heavenly minded they are of no earthly good." While I understand the sentiment behind this statement, such a condition is actually impossible. Indeed, there are some who are so earthly minded that they are of no heavenly good! But I have also met people who are out of touch with practical life and call it "being spiritual." Because of wounding, they wear a mask of super-spirituality and hide behind pretension. It may be true that they are of no earthly good, but it is not because they are too heavenly minded. It is because they have not dealt with their issues. If we are truly heavenly minded we will be of the utmost earthly good, because God is love, and love is practical.

As our minds become genuinely "set on things above,"[1] we are transformed into people who make the maximum positive and practical impact in our environments. How much more practical can we get than doing what we see the Father doing?[2] What could be more practical than doing greater works than Jesus:[3] doing good things and healing people who are oppressed by the devil?[4] Those who press into this type of heavenly minded/earthly goodness are the ones who will fulfill the longing of all creation for the revealing of the sons of God![5] When we are truly heavenly minded, we are a blessing to this planet. We are called to be living demonstrations of the goodness of God that leads people to repentance.

God does not invite His Church to spiritual encounters for impractical reasons. He is not releasing these precious gifts to

---

[1] Colossians 3:1
[2] John 5:19
[3] John 14:12
[4] Acts 10:38
[5] Romans 8:19

those who will bury them in the ground of a meaningless and disconnected spirituality. God is moving us from glory to glory[1] with a very concentrated intentionality. The practical implications of supernatural revelation are ours to discover.

One challenge for the Body of Christ in the days to come will be humility in the midst of increasing dimensions of supernatural power and revelation. Beware: Having significant experiences does not make us better than anyone else. Teresa of Avila, a sixteenth century Carmelite nun, had many angelic encounters and mystical experiences. She concluded that God gave her these experiences because she was weak and needed them to help her feeble faith. Our experience may be profound, but the more profound the experience, the more it should draw us closer to our brothers and sisters in humble gratitude, rather than isolating us in pride.

If you are tempted toward pride, you probably are not aware of it! But if supernatural encounters lead you into pride, please remember: you did not do anything to earn the encounter. We cannot strive or drive ourselves into the third heaven. We simply open our hearts to the Spirit of the Lord.

I did not merit it. It was freely given because of God's good pleasure. It was given despite my fear, my flaws and my lack of understanding. But it was also given because of the "yes" that resided within me. All of God's children have infinite favor. One is not over another or better than another. **Gifts always reflect the character of the giver more than the receiver.** Heavenly encounters are not spiritual scout badges that we earn and sew onto the sash of pride. They are reflections of God's

---

[1] 2 Corinthians 3:18

127

goodness, His willingness to associate with the lowly and to help the faith of the weak!

Ultimately, these experiences are custom-tailored to intensify our love affair with Jesus. In His Kingdom, everything rises and falls upon intimacy. **Everything.**

Astonishing as it may seem, God **wants** us to see His face. Intimacy with His people is the predominate passion of His heart. All other loves are inferior substitutes. He greatly desires a people that are entirely His. There are very few things in the Kingdom that build genuine, sustained passion for Jesus aside from personal revelatory encounters. The more I reflected on the encounter, the specific elements of it, and the fact that God revealed Himself to me, the more passion for intimacy filled my heart.

Thankfully, the message of intimacy with God is taking hold in the church. Intimacy is also one of God's masterfully designed processes. It allows us to advance in the gifts of the Spirit, and the gifts of the Spirit are springboards to deeper intimacy. Can we be intimate with God without seeing angels? The answer is a resounding, "Yes." But does it help our weak faith to interact with angels? Absolutely.

Having encountered an angel, having seen the Lion roar, having stood face to face with the risen Son of Man, Himself, I am ruined for this life. Everything now seems a little bland compared to heavenly realities. I **must** have more of Him. I have seen the King face to face and I want more. One glimpse has fueled an unquenchable, undeniable thirst for more! One brief encounter with Him has ignited a flame of desire that nothing can extinguish! And God is inviting more and more of His children to experience this.

In times past, before intimacy reclaimed the heart of the Church, talk of seeing angels and having encounters in the third heaven might have tempted some to become enamored with the experience, and stop short of deeper intimacy with Jesus. It may have even pressured some who are zealous to experience the supernatural to imagine these types of experiences, or worse, to fabricate such experiences. When we become more thrilled by these types of events than by God, Himself, we have missed the point entirely. His greatest desire is that we love Him and walk in deep intimacy with Him. How does this relate to how we process supernatural encounters of this sort?

When God started stirring up the prophetic in our church, we were so excited about hearing His voice! One day early in our corporate journey, God spoke to me very clearly, "It's good that you hear My voice, but I am bringing you to a place where I can direct you with my eyes." How intimate do you have to be with someone to be directed by their eyes?

Sometimes when I am preaching, I will come dangerously close to using an illustration my wife would think inappropriate. When I make eye contact with her, I can tell she is thinking, *Be careful how far you go with this story, buddy!* How do I know that? I have seen that look in her eyes before – many times! I know my wife's eyes! Having looked into the eyes of my Redeemer King, I now understand why God is excited for us to seek His face.

He **wants** us to see Him face to face. He **wants** to disclose Himself to us. When we ask for such encounters in the context of pursuing deeper intimacy, He welcomes our requests for Biblical revelatory experiences. He is excited, because He knows that when He answers these requests, the result will be an infusion of passion in the heart of His Bride.

Have you ever had passion for someone that was not fully reciprocated? Stinks, doesn't it? Did it make you wish you could do something to win the passion of the one you dreamed about? This is the way the end-time scenario will play out between the Lord and His Church. He is releasing supernatural encounters in order to stir our passion for Him. He is wild about us with extravagant love, and He has the power to "Wow" us and "Woo" us until we will reciprocate His extravagant love. He wants us to share in the excitement! The Lord, Himself, is accelerating our passion for Him by every available means!

As you recall from Chapter 5, as the encounter unfolded, eventually I was ushered into the presence of Jesus, Himself. As I stood there, I found myself looking into the face of a stranger. When I realized that I did not recognize Him, my heart broke, but not with condemnation. Instead, I realized it was a vast and significant invitation of grace. God repeatedly invites us to seek His face. In times past, I thought seeking his face was a figure of speech. Now, I am receiving grace to take that command literally. We must see His face! We must know His eyes! There is going to be a great wedding. Jesus is going to present to Himself a Bride without spot or wrinkle.[1] We will know our Bridegroom!

This is the ultimate purpose and end for all angelic encounters and supernatural experiences. God knows how fascinating He is. Because of His perfect self knowledge, He is

---

[1] Ephesians 5:27

supremely restful in the fact that to know Him is to love Him. This is precisely why He is stepping up the measure of revelation and demonstration: so that His people will be as wild about Him as He is about them!

I bless you to process your forthcoming supernatural encounters with careful attention and to steward every heavenly gift with great intentionality. This will allow the Lord to draw you into deeper places of intimacy that will transform every aspect of your life on earth.

Chapter 10
What Now?

Seal the book until the time of the end; many shall run to and fro, and knowledge shall increase.
Daniel 12:4

We live in a remarkable time in human history. The experiences we see and hear about are absolutely stunning: angelic activity, visions, dreams, healings and deliverances. As with my "suddenly", every encounter with the Lord has immense practical application. This marked increase in supernatural activity is one indicator that the church is entering a dramatic new season, one in which such supernatural signs and wonders will become more widespread, and more accessible. Many reading this book will be launched into a season of rapid increase in their own supernatural experiences. It is all happening in our lives right before our very eyes. I sometimes ask myself *why* such a prophetic season is exploding among "everyday" Christians. Why us? Why now?

My encounter is just one example of the acceleration of revelation being released from heaven in this season. These types of encounters have a very strategic and important practical application for the Body of Christ – and mine is no exception.

The encounter I have described has several timely applications:

- God is inviting all of us to allow His sword to lovingly, yet ruthlessly, circumcise our hearts. True freedom is available.

- The Lord Jesus has a fiery baptism for all of us. We can burn with passion for Him because He burns with passion for us.

- The fire of passion for the nations is available to all of us, as well as the fire of purity unto intimacy.

- The Lion of Judah is releasing his majestic roar so that all of us can press in for the dominion he created for us to exercise as kings and priests.

- God is calling all of us to live in such intimacy that we genuinely recognize His face. He longs for all of us to seek His face as the ultimate motivation of our lives.

- Finally, the Lord is calling His kids to live in supernatural unity. Working out relationships and unforgiveness is a strategic key to releasing the fire of God over entire regions.

In this third heaven experience, the messages were very practical and have proven to be a timely word from the Lord for this today. In fact, this testimony itself is becoming a launching pad for many others to experience heavenly realities on earth.

There are many "suddenlies of God" happening all around us. Permission has been granted for all of us to approach God desiring the experiences that are seen in Scripture. The Lord is inviting His church to come up higher and deeper, into areas that we have relegated to centuries long ago.

For what other purposes is God accelerating revelatory encounters in this hour?

First, there is a growing desperation for genuine spirituality. This observation is not just about those within the

133

church, but about those outside it as well. I am an avid reader of books for CEOs and business leaders. After reading many such books, it occurred to me that most successful CEOs practice some form of spirituality. Whether mediation, contemplative prayer, tai chi, or yoga, top CEOs are discovering that spirituality is necessary for achieving greatness in their arena of business. They spend millions learning new spiritual disciplines.

The impact of this is that their hunt for spirituality does not include the church of America – at least, not yet! Even so, they are craving genuine spiritual experience, and that desire is growing. *The multi-million dollar industry in spirituality simply means it is our moment to rise to our calling and answer this growing hunger.* God created Christians with the exclusive solution for spiritual hunger in every arena of life, including that of the Fortune 500 CEO.

God created humans with a desire for that which is exhilarating, extraordinary, and transcendent. Encoded in us is a longing for something that cannot be explained with logic alone. To say pre-Christians are spiritually hungry is a drastic understatement. In the 1970s and 80s, Hollywood and the popular media exposed the stirrings of a spiritual awakening with a wave of movies and TV shows with spiritual themes. Most of these were demonic, some produced in the name of "good, clean fun," but they revealed something quite significant. They indicated that the average consumer of popular culture had an underlying hunger for the supernatural.

Rather than taking the hint, the church's overall response was to denounce such entertainment as evil. *We responded to it as an assault instead of an invitation.* Instead of asking God what He was doing, we adopted a siege mentality and made a hasty retreat. So far, we have allowed the intense spiritual hunger

134

growing over the past several decades to be satisfied with inferior counterfeits. The hunger remains and intensifies even today.

My heart aches for all the deeply spiritual men and women who came into our churches hungry for authentic supernatural Christianity. Many of these have had personal experiences and encounters they could not explain. They flocked to our churches, but they were disappointed by an encounter with the god of Western Rationalism. They either gave up their pursuit of the supernatural or they hopelessly turned elsewhere.

But the tide is turning. This innate hunger for the supernatural is not a disheartening indicator of an increasingly evil society – far from it! Instead, it testifies that God is using every means at His disposal, even popular media, music and Hollywood images, to awaken a longing that says, *There is more*. The Church holds the answer to this heart cry! As God is allowing our society to get in touch with their deep unanswered need for authentic, spiritual encounters, at the same time, He is providing the only answer for this heart cry: an encounter with a Supernatural God who is alive and actively interfacing with humanity.

God is an amazing strategist! He is preparing pre-Christians by stimulating within them a genuine hunger that will be satisfied exclusively by the message and lifestyle He is developing in the church. This situation could not be more advantageous for the advancement of the Gospel of the Kingdom, and it is impossible to have been arranged by human strategy! God, Himself, has made the world hungry for what He is releasing! When this deep craving for the supernatural is met by God through a people fully engaged with Him in

135

extraordinary supernatural encounters, all counterfeits will lose their appeal.

Another reason we will see a marked increase in supernatural activity in our generation is found in Old Testament prophecies. Daniel's amazingly detailed prophecy of the end times predicts that in these last days, knowledge would increase.[1] But, in seeming contradiction, Solomon wrote that there is "nothing new under the sun."[2] In other words, everything that can be learned and discovered has already been learned and discovered. How can knowledge increase when everything there is to know under the sun is already known? Do these passages actually contradict each other?

Indeed, everything **under** the sun **has** already been discovered and learned. God is fulfilling Daniel's prediction by disclosing to us realities that exist **over** the sun. This is why the Lord's Prayer includes the phrase "on earth as it is in heaven."[3] ***God's answer to His Son's model prayer necessitates releasing supernatural phenomena from dimensions other than those we inhabit – dimensions over the sun!***

The supernatural properties of the Kingdom of Heaven are steadily pressing into the kingdoms of the world. In the Hebrew culture of the day, knowledge was synonymous with experience. So, our **knowledge** of God's supernatural realities is in fact, increasing as we **experience** His manifest presence in greater measures. Access to these previously inaccessible realms is now open to all believers.

---

[1] Daniel 12:9
[2] Ecclesiastes 1:9
[3] Matthew 6

◆◆◆

The knowledge of God's mysterious side is stimulating and exhilarating. I love the fact that I cannot wrap my brain around God. His mystery is an invitation for me to search Him out, to increase in the experience of Him, to discover His thoughts and His ways, and to enter into deeper revelation.

Mystery should not scare us. Most supernatural encounters leave us scratching our heads thinking, *What was that all about? I don't understand what just happened.* We don't have to answer every question raised by such experiences. "Religion" prides itself on answering every question. Spirituality is full of mystery. Intimacy with a mysterious God necessitates contentment with mystery. If you believe you can fully understand God, your god is way too small! Bill Johnson of Bethel Church in Redding, California, says it this way, "*If you had an encounter that did not raise more questions than answers, then you had an inferior encounter.*"

We will simply not be able to explain the supernatural experiences we are sure to have in the days to come. On our best day, we only know in part! There is much we will need angelic help to understand.

There will be a marked amplification in supernatural activity in the days to come. Daniel predicted such an outpouring of intimate, experiential knowledge in the last days. Revelation and demonstration are part and parcel of true experiential knowledge of God. Such knowledge will equip us to walk in power.

◆◆◆

This generation will witness a dramatic increase in supernatural activity, because God is raising our faith level for the invasion of His Kingdom on earth. As detailed in an earlier chapter, a friend reported that she heard a beautiful choir singing behind her during worship service. When she turned to see who it was, there was no one there. A couple of other people in that meeting heard the exact same thing. Because they heard angels singing audibly in one of our meetings, they do not need me to convince them of the reality of angelic ministry. It is no longer a stretch of faith for them to believe this. Because of their personal encounter, they will never be the same again. Why? Faith always increases with experience.

Whenever I see angels manifest in the natural, my faith cannot help but grow! Knowing that angels are sent by the Lord to do His word,[1] confidence overcomes my heart, because I know that Heaven is at work. There are certain angels I see whenever healings break out in our midst. When I see these particular angels, my faith rises and I release words of knowledge. At that moment, it is not a desperate hope that God would move in healing; it is a confident faith.

Why did angels manifest on earth in the scriptures? They usually came to announce something. Moreover, they usually came to announce a major change. When God was about to execute a major shift in the earth, angels started showing up! Their opening line was usually "Fear not...." Angels would appear so that faith would be built, because what was to occur next would have normally caused fear. We are going to need a lot of heavenly help to go where God is taking the church. The

---

[1] Psalm 103:21

shift is so great; the change is so monumental, that all of heaven is getting in on it!

Some parts of the church have prayed for these encounters for years. Every now and then, some really anointed person had an angelic visitation. But now, more and more of the body of Christ – everyday Christians – are starting to see angels with their physical eyes. This indicates that God is about to execute a major shift on this planet. As in the days when scripture was being written, by Daniel, by the disciples, by the early church, God is now telegraphing a major shift, which is why more people are beginning to see angels with their natural eyes.

There is no question that demons can have a significant negative impact on people. While Christians cannot be **possessed**, they can be demonized, or greatly affected by demons. In fact, the only demons I have ever dealt with directly have been among Christians. Knowing that demons are merely fallen angels, there is a surprising question that can be raised. If people can be demonized, then it would stand to reason that they can also be **angelized**. If this is true, then the angels of heaven, like fallen angels of hell, can directly influence the behavior and attitudes of Christians and pre-Christians. Those living in rebellion can be influenced by fallen angels; those living in submission to the Holy Spirit can be influenced by heaven's angels. At very least, it is a great possibility to ponder! But the truth is that our destiny is so great that we are going to need all of heaven's help!

Everything is shifting. Everything is moving. God's Kingdom is advancing and invading earth. Faith is rising within us. We **can** take signs and wonders wherever we go. We **can** usher in a great cultural perfusion of His Kingdom, one in which every institution of society will be impacted. This is no longer only for those on the platform – it is for all of us. If the "kingdom" we know only works in the confines of our church walls, it does not work at all! The Kingdom of Heaven is within reach, and it works wherever we go.

We must have a dramatic increase in faith! If we don't, we will be left like Elisha's servant when they were surrounded by the Syrian army. "Elisha, there's an army in our front yard. What are we going to do?" Elisha calmly replied, "Oh man, if only you could see that there are more on our side than on their side!"[1]

What would our faith be like if our eyes were open, like Elisha's servant, to see the myriads of angelic chariots? As we stand in obedience preparing to step out for the Kingdom, the enemy tries to intimidate. But when we see that there are more for us than against us, boldness, courage and radical steps of obedience follow. When we realize angels are present, who would back away from the fight? We will not be the least bit afraid of the devil or what he can do, because we know we have angelic help.

We are in a time of unprecedented warfare in which it will be absolutely essential for us to see and to be aware of the angelic hosts surrounding us. It would be foolish to worship angels, but it would be equally foolish to ignore them.

---

[1] 2 Kings 6:15

Some may wonder why angelic ministry is even necessary if the omnipotent God resides within us. In the same vein of inquiry, we can also ask why God uses human beings to do something that He can do without our help! Welcome to the realm of mystery!

Whether or not we understand angelic activity, the truth is we must have angelic help. If we continue looking at life without heaven's perspective, we will most likely get discouraged and depressed. When God opens our eyes to see that there are more for us than against us, hell does not stand a chance! The gates of hell will never withstand a church marching against them, fully confident that heaven's host is marching with us! Those gates will not prevail – **they cannot prevail.**

There is another reason why supernatural activity is becoming more accessible to the Church in these days. *The kingdoms of this world are about to become kingdoms of our Lord.* Jesus is about to be enthroned literally and physically as he is enthroned in the hearts of believers. We are co-heirs to the throne, and we are being prepared to reign. Our Father is about to turn over the family estate to His family. He is about to transfer to us the executorship of this planet.

Knowing this is true, as we approach the final days, consider this: How many would call their toddlers into the study and show them their will, their safe-deposit box or how they have structured their portfolio? Good fathers normally show the intricate inner-workings of their estate, not to their toddlers, but to their grown children, just before they are about to transfer it into their hands. This comes only after years of sonship. An heir

141

to the family estate earns trust by being faithful with increasing amounts of responsibility. Eventually, they can be entrusted with the entire estate. At that point, the "behind the scenes" information is released so that they can take over.

As co-heirs with Jesus, we are destined for co-regency. We will rule this planet with our eternal Partner, but before He turns the estate over to us, He is showing us the intricate inner-workings of the Kingdom of Heaven.

Spiritual activity will increase, because the Holy Spirit is restoring the church to "normal." Leonard Ravenhill said "The church is so **subnormal** if it ever became **normal** it would appear **abnormal**." Given all we are experiencing, many Christians might be tempted to think the new **normal** is a little weird. According to our current post-enlightenment definition of **weird**, much of the Bible fits that category as well! What is normal about walking around naked and barefoot for three years like Isaiah?[1] What is normal about Balaam's donkey turning around and telling him to quit hitting her?[2] What is normal about guys rowing a boat during a storm and seeing someone walking toward them across the waves?[3] What is normal about Hosea, an ordained minister, marrying a practicing prostitute?[4]

It seems that our idea of **normal** must be challenged in order for the supernatural to once again take root and flourish. I once heard a Christian leader say of the Toronto revival, "If people get uncomfortable with a little falling down, laughing and

---

[1] Isaiah 20
[2] Numbers 22
[3] Matthew 14
[4] Hosea 1

shaking, they're really going to freak out over blood, fire and columns of smoke predicted by the prophet Joel."[1] The supernatural is – **super**-natural. It transcends the natural.

When I say that the church is being **normalized** into increased levels of supernatural activity, I do not mean that supernatural experience is in anyway plain, ordinary or pedestrian. I simply mean that supernatural experience is **accessible** to the rank and file believer. Such occurrences will become more frequent and common, but they will never be ordinary or familiar.

One of my favorite snapshots of our new **normal** is the account of Peter's jailbreak.[2] In Acts 12, we find Peter in prison when an angel suddenly appears. The angel physically opens the cell door, leads him out, and then disappears. Peter wakes up from what he thought was a dream, in the middle of a dusty street. When he figures out he was not dreaming or having a vision, he walks to the meeting where believers were praying for his release. While at the gate, a servant girl named Rhoda recognizes his voice, and rushes back into the prayer meeting without even letting Peter in. "Hey everyone! The guy you're praying for is at the door!" she exclaims. Astonished, they reply, "No way! It's not Peter – it is his angel."

This account strikes me as humorous and challenging because, while the early church saw many prayers answered, **it was easier for them to believe <u>an angel was at the gate</u> than to believe that God would answer their prayer and get Peter out of jail!** Angelic visitations must have been frequent. In fact,

---

[1] Joel 2:30
[2] Acts 12

143

they were so normal that Rhoda didn't open the gate. (A word to the wise: if an angel knocks on your front door, please open it!) Apparently that church was so accustomed to angels physically manifesting that Rhoda unquestioningly thought one was at the gate. Now **that** is weird - and yet it was **normal** for the church of the first century. God, help us become normal again!

God is tearing back the veil that has kept us ordinary folks from entering into supernatural realities. Nothing stands between you and deeper revelation. Nothing stands between you and an open heaven – at least not on God's part.

My life has radically been wonderfully rearranged through this encounter. The message that it contained, and the event itself, have resulted in a season of acceleration that is absolutely staggering. My life is not the same. Our church is not the same. We are more in love with the Lord Jesus, deeper in the Word, more full of praise and thanksgiving, than ever. God is amazingly good!

What began as a normal mission trip, resulted in thousands of lives being transformed in tremendous ways. It also resulted in you reading this book. My prayer is that God launches you into even greater encounters in the Spirit. May you encounter a suddenly of God leaving you forever changed. May your church enter a season of unprecedented favor and revelation. May you and your spiritual family radically impact your local communities. May you never settle for a "good Christian experience" when God has put a calling for something great within you! I bless you to go for it! I pray that all I have described, all that was released to me on that normal Wednesday, would be transferred to you right now. I pray that your eyes

144

would be flooded with revelation and that you would see the heavenly hosts around you. There are more for you than against you!

The Lord is saying: "Anyone who is hungry; anyone who will steward and value deeper revelation; anyone who wants to have more – can have more." He is opening the eyes of His people **indiscriminately**! He runs to meet those who open their hearts, adjust their lives, and simply pray, ***Lord, I must have more.***